Managing People in Small and Medium Enterprises in Turbulent Contexts

Managing People in Small and Medium Enterprises in Turbulent Contexts explores a range of human resource management (HRM) issues specific to small and medium-sized enterprises (SMEs). Based on a series of research studies and secondary sources of data, the book's primary aim is to contextualise HRM issues in SMEs operating in a variety of national economic contexts that are (or have recently experienced) a turbulent situation. SMEs are the backbone of these economies. It is therefore critical that we study HR practices and concepts within such enterprises. The book covers HR practices in SMEs, such as recruitment and selection, training and development, performance evaluation and employee relations, by focusing on three types of turbulent economies: emerging market economies in Asia, the Pacific, Africa and Latin America; transition economies of Central and Eastern Europe; and crisis contexts in Southern Europe.

Managing People in Small and Medium Enterprises in Turbulent Contexts is a useful resource for organisations, practitioners, academics and scholars in the fields of HRM, employee engagement, small and medium business management and other related disciplines.

Alexandros Psychogios is a Professor of International HRM at Birmingham City University, UK.

Rea Prouska is an Associate Professor of HRM at London South Bank University, UK.

Routledge Studies in Small Business

Edited by Robert Blackburn, Director of The Small Business Research Centre, Kingston University, UK

For more information about this series, please visit: https://www.routledge.com

Managing People in Small and Medium Enterprises in Turbulent Contexts

Alexandros Psychogios and
Rea Prouska

NEW YORK AND LONDON

First published 2019
by Routledge
605 Third Avenue, New York, NY 10017

and by Routledge
2 Park Square, Milton Park, Abingdon, Oxon, OX14 4RN

First issued in paperback 2021

Routledge is an imprint of the Taylor & Francis Group, an informa business

Library of Congress Cataloging-in-Publication Data
Names: Psychogios, Alexandros, author. | Prouska, Rea, author.
Title: Managing people in small and medium enterprises in turbulent contexts / Alexandros Psychogios and Rea Prouska.
Description: New York, NY: Routledge, 2019. |
Series: Routledge studies in small business | Includes index.
Identifiers: LCCN 2018048187
Subjects: LCSH: Small business—Developing countries—Personnel management. | Small business—Developing countries—Management.
Classification: LCC HF5549.2.D48 P79 2019 |
DDC 658.3—dc23
LC record available at https://lccn.loc.gov/2018048187

ISBN 13: 978-0-367-78691-5 (pbk)
ISBN 13: 978-1-138-10355-9 (hbk)

Typeset in Sabon
by codeMantra

Contents

Author Biographies

Alexandros Psychogios is Professor of International HRM at Birmingham City University, UK. He is an affiliated researcher of the South-Eastern European Research Centre. His research interests are associated with International HRM, leadership with a focus on behavioural and neuroscience aspects, HRM practices in SMEs and project-based organisations, complexity and change and the human side of quality management practices. He has published his work in various academic journals, such as the *British Journal of Management, The International Journal of HRM, Employee Relations, Industrial Relations, Personnel Review* and *Economic and Industrial Democracy.*

Rea Prouska is Associate Professor of HRM at London South Bank University, UK. She is an Academic Member of the Chartered Institute of Personnel and Development and a Senior Fellow of the Higher Education Academy. Her research interests fall within the area of HRM from an international and comparative perspective, particularly on how economic crisis and transition affects work, employment and HR practices in small and medium-sized enterprises. She has published her work in various academic journals, such as the *British Journal of Management, Economic and Industrial Democracy, The International Journal of HRM, European Management Review, Employee Relations* and *Personnel Review.*

List of Figures

List of Abbreviations

BRIC	Brazil, Russia, India, China
CEE	Central and Eastern Europe
CEO	Chief Executive Officer
CME	Coordinated Market Economy
ER	Employee Relations
FDI	Foreign Direct Investment
GDP	Gross Domestic Product
EC	European Commission
EME	Emerging Market Economy
EU	European Union
HR	Human Resources
HRD	Human Resource Development
HRM	Human Resource Management
ILO	International Labour Organisation
IMF	International Monetary Fund
LME	Liberal Market Economy
MNC	Multinational Corporation
NSBD	National Small Business Development
OECD	Organisation for Economic Co-operation and Development
SME	Small and Medium-Sized Enterprise
TU	Trade Union
USSR	Union of Soviet Socialist Republics

1 Introduction

Purpose and Context of the Book

This book explores a range of human resource management (HRM) issues specific to small and medium-sized enterprises (SMEs). Based on a series of research studies and secondary sources of data, the book's primary aim is to contextualise HRM issues in SMEs operating in a variety of national economic contexts that are (or have recently experienced) a turbulent situation. We adopt a generic definition of turbulent contexts, referring to contexts that are characterised by a turbulent sociopolitical and historical environment and, subsequently, weak institutional bases. In particular, we refer to an entire process of continued and long-term economic shift of a country facing high level of uncertainty, volatility and structural change. We use the term 'turbulent' to describe various economies that are either under development, transformation, transition or under crisis. We use the term to describe three similar but also different types of contexts, namely emerging market economies, transition economies and crisis economies.

SMEs are the backbone of these economies. It is therefore critical that we study HR practices and concepts within such enterprises. Therefore, the book covers HR practices in SMEs, such as recruitment and selection, training and development, performance evaluation and employee relations, by focusing on three types of turbulent economies: (i) emerging markets, particularly Asia and the Pacific (China, India, Taiwan, Vietnam, Indonesia and South Korea), Africa (South Africa, Ghana, Nigeria and Algeria) and Latin America (Chile and Colombia); (ii) transition economies of Central and Eastern Europe (Poland, Hungary, the Czech Republic, Slovenia, Bulgaria); and (iii) crisis contexts in Southern Europe (Greece, Italy and Spain). The book is a useful resource for organisations, practitioners, academics and scholars. In the following sections, we explain the approach to SMEs we adopt, as well as describe in more detail the three types of turbulent contexts this book focuses on.

What Is Meant by 'Small and Medium-Sized Enterprises'

SMEs are non-subsidiary, independent firms which employ less than a given number of employees, with this number varying between countries

(OECD, 2005). In the European Union (EU), the European Commission recommendation (96/280/EC) of 3 April 1996 [Official Journal L 107 of 30.04.1996] defines organisational size of these companies as follows: micro (less than ten employees); small (10–49 employees); medium (50–249 employees); and large (more than 250 employees). However, some countries set the limit at 200 employees, while the US considers SMEs to include firms with fewer than 500 employees (OECD, 2005). Small firms are generally those with fewer than 50 employees, while microenterprises have at most ten employees (OECD, 2005).

The number of employees, however, is not the only element used to define SMEs. Financial assets are also used to define organisational size. In the EU, a new definition came into force on 1 January 2005 (OECD, 2005): medium-sized enterprises are defined as having a turnover of up to EUR 50 million; small enterprises as having a turnover of up to EUR 10 million; and micro firms as having a turnover of no more than EUR 2 million. Alternatively, balance sheets for medium, small and microenterprises should not exceed EUR 43 million, EUR 10 million and EUR 2 million, respectively. For the purposes of this book and due to the variety of regions under examination, we adopt the OECD (2005) definition of SMEs based on number of employees and include organisations with fewer than 500 employees. However, we do acknowledge that in some regions we study, such as countries in the EU, the usual SME size is defined as having fewer than 250 employees. With this broad definition, we include companies from all around the world that operate in a more or less similar manner. Therefore, it would be interesting to explore what kind of HRM practices these companies adopt given the turbulent environment within which these organisations operate.

Turbulent Contexts

As argued earlier, these turbulent contexts include countries that can be considered emerging economies, as well as emerging economies that are under political and economic (and in some cases social) transition. In addition, our definition of 'turbulent contexts' includes economies (mainly developed) that have passed through a financial crisis impacting on SMEs and on HRM practices. The following sections explain in brief each one of these three categories of turbulent contexts. Detailed analysis about each of them can be found at the beginning of the relevant chapters in this book.

Emerging Market Economies

Emerging market economies (EMEs) are defined as those countries whose competitive advantages measured by the shares of GDP, exports and outward foreign direct investment in the world are higher than the average competitiveness advantages of all countries except developed countries (Kim and Jung, 2009). An emerging market is a country that shares some of the characteristics of a developed market, but does not quite satisfy all requirements to be termed a developed market. The four largest emerging economies are the BRIC countries (Brazil, Russia, India and China). In this book, we explore a selection of emerging economies based on available research. The regions we focus on are Asia and the Pacific (China, India, Taiwan, Vietnam, Indonesia and South Korea), Africa (South Africa, Ghana, Nigeria and Algeria) and Latin America (Chile and Colombia).

Transition Economies

Since the 1990s, a number of peripheral European countries are in a process of political and economic transition from centrally planned (socialist) economies to capitalist ones. The countries that used to belong either to the Union of Soviet Socialist Republics (USSR) block or to the Yugoslav state have undergone a set of structural transformations (Feige, 2017). They are well known as *ex-communist* or *post-communist* countries, and they have been classified as 'transition economies' (Stark and Bruszt, 1998). In this book, we particularly explore countries of the Central and Eastern European periphery, specifically Poland, Hungary, the Czech Republic, Slovenia and Bulgaria.

Crisis Economies

The 2008 global economic crisis affected many European economies, particularly those in Southern Europe. We define crisis economies as those hit by this economic crisis. A decade after this crisis started, many European nations are still struggling to return to pre-crisis levels (Le Monde, 2018). We therefore explore three countries in more detail in this book: Greece, Italy and Spain. The economic crisis created turbulent market conditions that severely affected SMEs in these economies. This book explores the impact that the crisis had on these economies and on people management in SMEs.

The Importance of Small and Medium-Sized Enterprises for Turbulent Economies

There is broad agreement that SMEs are vital to achieving decent and productive employment, as they globally account for two-thirds of all jobs and are responsible for the creation of new jobs (ILO, 2015). The importance of SMEs is even more critical for emerging, transition and crisis economies (The World Bank, 2013). However, the social-economic environment in such economies differs significantly from that in developed economies in terms of institutional framework, norms, resources and infrastructures (Han and Xiang, 2017; Psychogios and Wood, 2010; Psychogios et al., 2016).

SMEs contribute to all sectors and industries – from agriculture to manufacturing and services – and they create jobs at a faster rate compared to larger companies. SMEs expand productive capability and help absorb productive resources at all levels of the economy, which creates flexibility in economic systems that allows the collaboration between small and large companies (Subhan et al., 2013). This enhances foreign direct investments of large, usually multinational firms.

SMEs in emerging, transition and crisis economies contribute positively to the formulation of both political and social environments in these countries, enhancing changes and modernisation of the system where possible (McIntyre, 2001). SMEs absorb both material and human resources from larger firms while reformulating labour market conditions, ensuring a balancing process between them and larger companies (McIntyre, 2001). In this respect, SMEs are embedded in the institutional structures of these economies (Granovetter, 1985). SMEs also contribute to the economic development through creation of employment opportunities for growth of both rural and urban labour forces, provision of sustainability and innovation to the whole economy (Subhan et al., 2013). SMEs have a significant impact on income distribution, tax revenue, employment, family income stability and effective utilisation of resources. They have the ability to employ more labour-intensive production processes compared to large companies (Subhan et al., 2013). In low-income economies, SMEs account for 60% of gross domestic product (GDP) and 70% of total employment, and in middle-income economies, they contribute 70% of GDP and 95% of total employment (Subhan et al., 2013). Overall, SMEs have the ability to provide productive employment opportunities, generate income and contribute to the reduction of poverty in emerging economies.

Despite their potential to contribute to the world economy, SMEs face many challenges (Newberry, 2006). The Economist Intelligence Unit (EIU) (2009) reported inadequate access to financial resources and investment capital as significant barriers to growth for these companies in emerging, transition and crisis economies. Recent changes in the global economy due to the 2008 global financial crisis and the 2009–2010 Eurozone crisis had, and in many cases still have (as of this book's writing in 2018), an impact on SMEs in these economies. SMEs have been exposed to global competition from other SMEs and large multinational corporations (MNCs). The intense internationalisation of SMEs forced them to become more innovative in order to enhance their competitive advantage. In a similar vein, they need to find ways (again innovative) to cut costs and improve efficiency. At the same time, another challenge relates to their ability to invest in research and development. A recent study found that only about 3% of SMEs invested in research and development of new technologies and products, while over 80% of them are followers of technologies usually developed by large companies (Khazragui, 2011). The latter has an impact on their internationalisation process since they lack the necessary resources and technological advancements.

These challenges have a negative impact on the survival of SMEs, leading to high failure rates in many economies around the globe, including in developed and emerging economies (Switzer and Huang, 2007). The result is the emergence of various business management approaches that seek to help SME development and growth in developed countries (Newberry, 2006). In parallel, many of these practices are transferred to SMEs in emerging, transition and crisis economies. However, there is a lot of research questioning the applicability of such management practices in SMEs, particularly from Western contexts to non-Western contexts (e.g. Psychogios et al., 2010).

In short, SMEs in turbulent contexts play a critical role for both the economy and society in these countries. SMEs provide employment opportunities, generate income and contribute to the reduction of poverty in emerging economies. While opportunities for SMEs have emerged during the last decade, especially after the global financial crisis, there are still many challenges that SMEs face. It is more difficult for them to capitalise on potential opportunities due to a lack of institutional support and resources. In this respect, human resources are considered extremely important for SMEs operating in turbulent contexts since they can provide the appropriate competitive advantage through their knowledge and experience, especially when these companies cannot invest a lot in developing new technologies and innovations.

It is widely known that SMEs around the world rely on less formal HRM practices (Psychogios et al., 2016). The reason for this is twofold. First, most SMEs cannot afford the investment in HRM. This means that they cannot maintain and develop HRM departments staffed with HRM professionals and experts. They prefer to either outsource specific HR functions (payroll, training, etc.) or use more informal pillars of when applying practices (performance evaluation, etc.). Second, the dominant role of the owner within these companies (usually the CEO) affects HRM application. The owner/CEO is in charge of HRM decisions. SME owners/CEOs create an informal context within these organisations. For example, in selection practices, SMEs rely heavily on *word of mouth* and references rather than on formal and well-documented processes. There is also a lack of formal job descriptions in these firms. Furthermore, employee relations in SMEs differ from larger firms in many ways. For example, it is rare to find trade unions or collective bargaining in SMEs. The culture in these firms is typically moulded by the owners/CEOs of the firm, who directly communicate organisational objectives to employees. This creates an informal and flexible working environment. However, it seems that HRM development is not the same in all SMEs and especially in those operating in emerging, transition or crisis contexts. In this respect, this book attempts to map the current state of affairs of HRM in SMEs in turbulent contexts.

Overview of Chapters

The book comprises eight chapters. Chapter 2 explores the SME approach to HRM and provides a brief overview of how SMEs apply core HR practices. The chapter analyses the informal, emergent and reactive approach of managing people in SMEs. HRM in SMEs is usually performed by the owner or senior manager. SMEs do not usually have internal HR expertise or skills, but as organisational size increases, HR policies and practices become more formalised, and the presence of an HR function and/or department is more likely. The chapter explores how SMEs manage specific core HR practices, such as HR planning, talent management, resourcing, training and development, employee relations, performance management and reward systems.

Chapter 3 is the first of three chapters exploring HRM in SMEs in EMEs. EMEs are economies progressing towards becoming more advanced, usually by means of rapid growth and industrialisation. EMEs are not homogenous, although they do share similarities in terms of the historical development of their political, social and economic context. At the same time, EMEs have major societal and cultural differences that influence management practices. Within this context, this chapter focuses on EMEs in Asia and the Pacific, particularly on the role of SMEs and HRM in China, India, Taiwan, Vietnam, Indonesia and South Korea. In China, we found evidence of modernisation and formalisation of HRM and employment practices in SMEs due to the internationalisation of businesses in recent years. Similarly, we found that SMEs in India are progressively experiencing an accelerated growth in the use of HRM practices, such as training and development and talent management. However, in Taiwan, HRM application is limited due to cultural factors and to the high proportion of family-owned enterprises that rely on informal systems of management. In Vietnam, HRM formalisation in SMEs depends upon several factors, such as competition from international firms and state-owned enterprises, expectations from international business partners or customers, and pressure from banks. Finally, in South Korea, there is evidence of HRM formalisation; however, this is not consistent across enterprises.

Chapter 4 explores HRM in SMEs in some emerging economies located in Africa (South Africa, Ghana, Nigeria and Algeria). Although there is not much empirical evidence on South African SMEs and the HR practices they use, available research points to a need for a greater emphasis on competitiveness, managerial skills and training, and retention strategies for skilled workers. In Ghana, we found that SMEs apply some core HR practices, such as recruitment, selection and training. Other HR activities such as reward management, performance management, talent management and HR development are considered as less strategic. In Nigeria, SMEs depict a mix of HRM formality and informality depending on their industry. Historical and institutional factors have affected the presence of HRM practices in businesses, with some distinctive differences observed between SMEs and larger organisations. Similarly, strong historical, cultural and institutional factors have shaped HRM application in SMEs in Algeria. The greatest effect is observed in recruitment and selection practices that are mainly influenced by networking and nepotism.

Chapter 5 explores HRM in SMEs in emerging economies in Latin America. There is scarce research on HRM in SMEs in countries in this region. For this reason, this chapter focuses on Chile and Colombia, for which some research is available. The chapter briefly presents the historical background of these two emerging economies and discusses the nature of HRM in SMEs. HR practices in SMEs in Chile are primarily informal. There are strong cultural and institutional forces that prohibit small companies from following modern management practices, including HRM practices. In Colombia, small and medium organisations struggle between formality and informality of HRM. Formalisation in SMEs seems to stem from laws and regulations organisations need to abide by. The overall state of HRM can be considered underdeveloped, and more research is needed to understand various aspects of HRM practice and application in SMEs in these countries.

Chapter 6 explores HRM in SMEs in transition economies of Central and Eastern Europe. The past autarchic environment of state control in these countries means that entrepreneurial development has been slow and foreign investments limited. MNCs operating in the market can influence management thinking and practices in local SMEs. However, the owner usually manages SMEs in these countries, and for this reason, they develop their own informal way of working based on resources and expertise. Unregulated informal economic activities are a common feature in this region. This chapter discusses that smaller businesses in these economies do not have formalised HRM functions. However, there are three antecedents of HRM formalisation in SMEs operating in a post-communist context: degree of internationalisation, sector and size.

Chapter 7 explores the challenges the economic crisis posed for SMEs operating in European countries challenged the most by the 2008 global financial crisis, namely Greece, Italy and Spain. Many SMEs struggled for survival in increasingly turbulent markets. Their heavy dependence on credit and their inability to access finance when they needed it the most created a trade deficit between them and their suppliers, with spillover effects on employees. SMEs struggled to overcome the economic crisis due to their inability to downsize and diversify products/services and due to their weak financial structures and limited access to finance. As a response to these impediments, SMEs had to cut labour costs by freezing recruitment, downsizing, implementing pay cuts and layoffs. This context led to the intensification of adverse working conditions for employees in SMEs, making their working lives prone to job insecurity, work intensification and pressure. As a result, employee productivity, loyalty and commitment exhibited a decline.

Chapter 8 concludes this book by revisiting the current state of affairs of HRM in SMEs in turbulent contexts. The purpose of this chapter is to draw a conceptual model of HRM by highlighting the factors affecting HRM application in emerging, transition and crisis contexts. The chapter ends by offering practical implications and suggesting avenues for future research.

References

EIU (2009). *Surviving the drought: Access to finance among small and medium-sized enterprises.* Economist Intelligence Unit. [online]. Available at: http://graphics.eiu.com/upload/eb/Surviving_the_drought_WEB_2610.pdf. [Accessed 9 September 2018].

Feige, E. L. (2017). The transition to a market economy in Russia: Property rights, mass privatisation and stabilisation. In G. S. Alexander and G. Skapska, eds., *A Fourth Way? Privatisation, Property and the Emergence of New Market Economics.* Oxon: Routledge, pp. 81–102.

Granovetter, M. (1985). Economic action and social structure: The problem of embeddedness. *American Journal of Sociology*, 91(3): pp. 481–510.

Han, L. and Xiang, X. (2017). Emerging economies and financing of SMEs. In A. Woldie and B. Thomas, eds., *Financial Entrepreneurship for Economic Growth in Emerging Nations.* Hershey, PA: IGI Global.

ILO (2015). *Small and medium-sized enterprises and decent and productive employment creation.* Report IV. International Labour Conference, 104th session. [online]. Available at: www.ilo.org/wcmsp5/groups/public/—ed_norm/—relconf/documents/meetingdocument/wcms_358294.pdf. [Accessed 9 September 2018].

Khazragui, H. (2011). *Export promotion of small and medium-sized enterprises in developing countries: The perceived usefulness of international trade points by SMEs in Egypt.* [Thesis]. Manchester, UK: The University of Manchester.

Kim, Z. and Jung, M. (2009). Theoretical approach to define emerging markets and emerging market global companies: Double triangle model. *International Area Studies Review*, 12(1): pp. 1–15.

Le Monde (2018). La crise de 2008 a nourri les pupulismes europeens, 16 September 2018.

McIntyre, R. (2001). *The role of small and medium enterprises in transition: Growth and entrepreneurship.* World Institute for Development Economics Research. [online]. Available at: http://citeseerx.ist.psu.edu/viewdoc/download?doi=10.1.1.620.5142&rep=rep1&type=pdf. [Accessed 9 September 2018].

Newberry, D. (2006). *The role of small and medium-sized enterprises in the futures of emerging economies.* [online]. Available at: http://earthtrends. wri.org/features/view feature.php?theme=5&fid=69. [Accessed 9 September 2018].

OECD (2005). *SME and Entrepreneurship Outlook.* Paris: OECD.

Psychogios, A. G., Szamosi, L. T., Prouska, R. and Brewster, C. (2016). A three-fold framework for understanding HRM practices in South-Eastern European SMEs. *Employee Relations*, 38(3): pp. 310–331.

Psychogios, A. G., Szamosi, L. T. and Wood, G. (2010). Introducing employment relations in South Eastern Europe. *Employee Relations*, 32(3): pp. 205–211.

Psychogios, A. G. and Wood, G. (2010). Human resource management in Greece in comparative perspective: Alternative institutionalist perspectives and empirical realities. *The International Journal of Human Resource Management*, 21(14): pp. 2614–2630.

Stark, D. and Bruszt, L. (1998). *Postsocialist Pathways. Transforming Politics and Property in East Central Europe.* Cambridge: Cambridge University Press.

Subhan, Q. A., Mehmood, M. R. and Sattar, A. (2013). *Innovation in Small and Medium Enterprises (SMEs) and Its Impact on Economic Development in Pakistan.* Dubai, UAE: Proceedings of 6th International Business and Social Sciences Research Conference. ISBN: 978-1-922069-18-4.

Switzer, L. N. and Huang, Y. (2007). How does human capital affect the performance of small and mid-cap mutual funds? *Journal of Intellectual Capital*, 8(4): pp. 666–681.

The World Bank (2013). *SME Contributions to Employment, Job Creation, and Growth in the Arab World.* Middle East and North Africa Region, Financial and Private Sector Development Unit.

2   Human Resource Management Practices in SMEs

Introduction

There is a widespread belief that HRM concepts originating from research conducted in large multinational organisations can be universally applied in smaller organisational settings. This often leads to HRM practices, which are developed in large firms, to be uncritically applied within SMEs, neglecting that SMEs are different with respect to their institutional, resource and economic contexts. This chapter, therefore, explains the SME approach to HRM and provides a brief overview of how SMEs apply core HR practices. In particular, the first section of this chapter analyses the logic of HRM in SMEs by emphasising the nature of these organisations and how it affects HRM application. The sections that follow focus on core HR practices, such as HR planning, talent management, resourcing, training and development, employee relations, performance management and reward systems.

The SME Approach to Human Resource Management

When studying HRM in smaller firms, one might expect to find a scaled-down version of HRM practices existing in larger firms. However, this is not the case due to fundamental differences in their institutional, resource and economic contexts (Cassell et al., 2002; Cunningham, 2010; Krishnan and Scullion, 2017; Psychogios et al., 2016). Large organisations are more likely to adopt sophisticated staff resourcing strategies, offer higher extrinsic rewards and advanced career opportunities, develop and apply performance appraisal systems, demonstrate higher investment in training and development and have more developed internal labour markets (Krishnan and Scullion, 2017). The principle applied is that formality of HRM policies and practices increases with organisational size (Cardon and Stevens, 2004). However, HRM in SMEs takes a unique form, because SMEs are characterised by an informal, emergent and reactive approach in managing people (De Kok and Uhlaner, 2001; Harney and Dundon, 2006; Kotey and Slade, 2005; Marlow, 2000, 2002).

HRM in SMEs has been seen through either a 'small is beautiful' or a 'bleak-house' perspective (Wilkinson, 1999). On the one hand, the 'small is beautiful' perspective points out that less hierarchical/bureaucratic control builds up better social relations and makes it easier to change work assignments (Dietz et al., 2006). It assumes that SMEs develop healthier employee relations than larger organisations and possess more devoted and committed employees. Forth et al. (2006) argue that workers are highly satisfied by working in SMEs and that among the advantages is that they have a more pleasant work environment. In addition, Tsai et al. (2007) explain that job satisfaction in SMEs is achieved partly through informal employee relations. On the other hand, the 'bleak-house' perspective (Sisson, 1993) points out that the lack of formalised HR policies create a rather hostile environment for employees in SMEs. They face inadequate working conditions, poor health and safety, and have limited access to trade unions, leading to higher levels of potential conflict, higher turnover and more absenteeism (Rainnie, 1989). Since SMEs are not a homogenous category, there is evidence for both viewpoints. These two polarised perspectives have been labelled as exaggeratedly simplistic (Marlow, 2002) and the recent HRM literature is more nuanced.

This reliance on informal management practices (Behrends, 2007) has been attributed partly due to the owner's role in HRM decisions (Singh and Vohra, 2009) given the lack of formal HRM investment in small settings (Fabi et al., 2009; Marlow and Patton, 2002). Even when organisational size permits the presence of HRM specialists, it is still the owner, or managing director, who is generally seen to be in charge of HR decisions (Kroon et al., 2013), while HRM specialists are often seen to deal with administrative rather than strategic tasks (Edwards and Ram, 2009).

This informality in HRM means a lack of official HRM policies and procedures and an irregularity in their application (Nguyen and Bryant, 2004). Owners perceive HRM as an expensive and time-consuming bureaucracy (Bartram, 2005), and they are often seen to utilise informal and *ad hoc* HR practices in order to monitor employee performance (Wilkinson, 1999). SMEs may also avoid implementing formal HRM practices, because they do not possess the expertise and resources required (Marlow, 2002). In addition, the workforce skill-mix is a particularly strong influence on the extent to which a range of HRM practices are adopted in SMEs (Bacon and Hoque, 2005). This means that SMEs with a higher proportion of low-skilled workers are less likely to adopt certain HRM practices, whereas SMEs with a higher proportion of skilled workers are more likely to invest in such practices in order to retain and develop their talent (Psychogios et al., 2016).

Three key antecedents have been found to affect the formalisation of HRM practices in SMEs. First, the degree of internationalisation of SMEs and the extent to which they are linked to larger companies through strategic alliances and organisational networks may mean that SMEs come into contact with developed HRM practices (Psychogios et al., 2016) or that larger organisations operating abroad may have significant control over managerial decisions in SMEs (Bacon and Hoque, 2005). Second, organisational size affects the presence of HRM in SMEs, with larger organisations demonstrating a more formalised approach (Psychogios et al., 2016). Third, some sectors and industries, as for example manufacturing, appear to have a more formalised approach to HRM, especially because such sectors tend to be characterised by larger organisational sizes within the SME context (Psychogios et al., 2016). Alongside these antecedents, the business environment within which an SME operates is crucial. For example, Budhwar and Debrah (2001) discuss how different configurations of cultural, institutional, sector and business dynamics affect the impact of individual contingency factors (e.g. age, size, nature, life-cycle stage, level of technology, presence of unions and HRM strategies, business sector, stakeholders) on HRM policies and practices.

Despite the apparent lack of formalisation of HRM in SMEs, there is a generic and, in some cases, global argument that SMEs should develop a combination of different HRM practices. The reason is associated with mainly legal requirements and external pressures and expectations, in areas such as recruitment, selection, training and compensation in order to maintain business operations and follow international business trends (Cardon and Stevens, 2004). The remainder of this chapter explores the application of core HRM practices in SMEs.

HR Planning and Talent Management

A key aspect of HRM is resource planning. This is vital given the prevalence of SMEs in many countries. SMEs play an important role in reducing poverty and deprivation by providing employment, since large organisations are often incapable of generating sufficient employment opportunities. SMEs are, therefore, key to combating rise in unemployment globally. However, organisational structures and management processes in SMEs exhibit a great degree of instability in their organisational life cycle (Hanks and Chandler, 1994). As they grow in size and complexity, changing organisational structures make it challenging for them to systematically and strategically identify key positions and plan to fill these roles either through external recruitment (which is covered in the next section) or through internal recruitment by developing a talent pool (Krishnan and Scullion, 2017). The lack of strategic HR planning in SMEs is linked to the lack of strategic thinking within most of these companies that seems to be a critical issue (Stonehouse and Pemberton, 2002).

Talent management is a critical issue in SMEs although it is less developed. Although primary research in the field of talent management has focused more on MNEs (Stahl et al., 2012) or large domestic organisations, nowadays this focus includes different types of companies, like SMEs

(Tatoglu et al., 2016). Hunt (2017) points out that there is an increasing focus on the development of talent management in the private sector and especially in SMEs. Accordingly, Kontoghiorghes (2016) supports this view by arguing that the development of the talent management concept has become one of the main tools in achieving competitive advantage in SMEs in the last few years. Moreover, talent management is critical for SMEs that operate in a continuous changing, dynamic and turbulent business environment (Sharmila and Gopalakrishnan, 2013). Tyagarajan (2013) explains that in the last years companies are affected from the global problem called 'talent crisis', both in developed and emerging economies. The lack of talented workers leads to poor functioning of companies, sometimes even to their full closedown. In particular, he explains that a country's GDP can be increased if the national economy has a highly skilled workforce. Another way for SMEs to gain competitive advantage is through obtaining performance feedback for the highly qualified and talented workforce (Meutia and Bukhori, 2017), which links to the importance of developing an internal talent pool in SMEs.

When developing an internal talent pool, the SME approach to managing talent depends on the institutional and structural idiosyncrasies of this type of firms (Krishnan and Scullion, 2017). For example, research by Valverde et al. (2013) on Spanish medium-sized firms found an informal approach to talent management with little awareness of the term and rhetoric of talent management. Similarly, research by Kaliannan et al. (2016) on talent management in Malaysian SMEs found a gap between employees and employers in terms of expectations of talent management practices, with employees expecting better training than those provided by employers. On the contrary, research by Festing et al. (2013) on talent management in medium-sized German firms found a highly engaged and retention-based talent management approaches in the sample studied, indicating the strong long-term developmental orientation in the German national business system. The approach to talent management also varies according to organisational size. As firms evolve in size from very small to medium, there is a rapid increase in specialised jobs, hierarchical levels and functional divisions (Krishnan and Scullion, 2017), creating scope for managing talent in the firm. Finally, in their study, Sharmila and Gopalakrishnan (2013), through the analysis of several factors in SMEs (organisational culture and structure, freedom in the performance, diversity level, opportunity for innovation, dedication to work, ways of motivation), concluded that talent management could consist of the following steps: attracting talents, developing and promoting them and providing feedback on their work. They stress the close connection of successful leaders in SMEs with development of talent management, explaining that SME leaders need to understand the importance of talent management for their companies.

Employee Resourcing

Sustained competitive advantage can arise from the processes used to manage a firm's human capital (Barney, 1991). Yet 20% of SMEs in the EU identify 'availability of skilled staff or experienced managers' as the most pressing issue (European Commission, 2017). Employee turnover within small enterprises can have an enormous impact upon the survival of the business, especially when the business is located in rural and regional areas where it is hard to attract and recruit employees (Cameron et al., 2010). It has been argued that the goal in recruitment and selection in SMEs is to find the individual with the potential to best 'fit in' with the organisational culture. Making the wrong employment decisions can be costly for any business, particularly for smaller firms who have limited financial resources to engage in multiple recruitment rounds (Barrett et al., 2007). As the entire process of recruitment and selection in SMEs tends to be informal, less structured and less bureaucratic, the sourcing of candidates, according to Leung (2003), goes in the same direction. SME owners recruit based on their vision, without having a detailed job description or choosing to advertise their openings. They recruit from their personal network, based on feedback or prior experience with the recruit and the way the two communicated in that past context. As stated by Mayer-Haug et al. (2013), while enterprise grows, the entrepreneur enlarges the potential pool of candidates to the business network. Research has found that informal recruitment practices in SMEs frequently include the use of word of mouth and 'walk-ins' because they are perceived as convenient and inexpensive methods (Barrett et al., 2007; Carroll et al., 1999). Word of mouth is particularly important for SMEs as recruitment in small businesses can be conditional on the availability of a known individual (Atkinson and Meager, 1994). Research also suggests that employment decisions are likely to be made intuitively in small organisations (Lodato, 2008). In a similar vein, Bacon et al. (1996) posit that SME managers see psychometric tests as being unnecessary and time-consuming tools that are less effective compared to 'first impression' observations. Some argue that intuition is a bottom-up form of learning that is initially implicit but may eventually become explicit (Hodgkinson et al., 2008).

However, this means that such recruitment practices may lead to the employment of the wrong candidate because the larger pool of suitable candidates from the labour market remains untapped (Carroll et al., 1999). This informality in recruitment practices is considered problematic predominantly because it leaves the firm open to accusations of indirect discrimination in the selection process (Barrett et al., 2007). In addition, SMEs may also use internships for nurturing new talent (Cui et al., 2018). This means that they are more willing to invest time in developing talent internally in order to overcome the inherent issues with external recruitment.

While such informal recruitment practices may be utilised by SMEs, their sustainability in periods of growth, such as periods of expansion or diversification, is questionable since formal methods are needed to find appropriate employees from the labour market (Arthur, 1995; Barrett and Mayson, 2007; Kotey and Slade, 2005; Nguyen and Bryant, 2004). However, SMEs face challenges in attracting talent due to their limited visibility in comparison with larger organisations (Storey et al., 2010; Williamson et al., 2002). Potential applicants are often deterred from applying for work in SMEs because the perception is that salary, benefits, working conditions, training opportunities, career development and labour relations are less attractive than in larger organisations (Cardon and Stevens, 2004). Smaller firms are also perceived as fragile in an increasingly competitive business world (Storey, 1994), and this is another reason why potential applicants may be seeking employment in larger, more established and predictable firms (Reda and Dyer, 2010).

Despite a penchant for informality, recruitment methods in SMEs still differ by sectors or industries. SMEs have fewer resources and employees. It is therefore too complex for them to retain and grow an internal labour market centred on recruitment and career progression (Taylor, 2010). As a result, most SMEs employ flexible methods of recruitment (e.g. walk-in interviews) that are based on informal networking (Carroll et al., 1999).

Given the difficulties SMEs face in external recruitment and their vulnerability to competitive pressures (Mayson and Barrett, 2006), they are more likely to focus on utilising existing resources more efficiently and effectively (Festing et al., 2013). For example, research by Cameron et al. (2010) has found that smaller family-owned enterprises more often rely on the principle of relationship marketing for recruitment and retention. This principle refers to the development of partnerships between employers and employees through building trust and cooperation between the parties. The aim is to maximise relationships at work, therefore supporting retention, while new employees can be attracted to the organisations through building such relationships.

In terms of selection, few SME owners or managing directors have HR expertise in employee selection tools (Cardon and Stevens, 2004) or employ trained HR specialists (Kerr et al., 2007). Organisational structures are simple with few positions available, while roles are less well-defined and wide in scope (Reda and Dyer, 2010). Given the infrequency of the hiring process, employing HR professionals to assist with employee selection or investing in validated selection tests are not perceived as cost-effective solutions (Reda and Dyer, 2010). The most commonly used selection methods in SMEs is the 'classic trio': application forms, panel interviews and references (Stavrou-Costea and Manson, 2006). Other more advanced selection techniques such as psychometric tests and assessment centres are avoided due to their cost and time implications (Stavrou-Costea and Manson, 2006). In addition, SMEs sometimes outsource the recruitment function to external management consultants, such as headhunters or employment agencies, in order to access expertise and skills for the resourcing process (Galanaki and Papalexandris, 2005).

The effects of the recruitment and selection methods employed by SMEs can potentially lead to discrimination. Forth et al. (2006) argues that many SMEs fail to monitor equal opportunities in employment. This issue arises due to their informal approach to selection and due to the lack of internal knowledge of employment law. For instance, employers may fall into a pattern of recruiting one particular race that they are accustomed to (Ram and Holliday, 1993), while recruiting via word of mouth or personal recommendations hinders equal opportunities in resourcing.

Training and Development

SMEs provide less training compared to larger organisations. Litz and Stewart (2000) argue that training and development in SMEs is often informal and short-term oriented. Arguably, the type of work conducted in SMEs does not lend itself to formalised off-site training (Barrett, 2015). Large and medium-sized enterprises are more likely to provide external training to employees compared to small firms. In particular, research has found that SMEs are generally reluctant to invest in formal training methods (Billett et al., 2003; Westhead and Storey, 1996) and rather use informal and on-the-job approaches (Jones, 2010). It has been argued that the *ad hoc* use of training is due to a preconception that training is for new or less-experienced employees rather than seen as a continuous process of learning (Fuller-Love, 2006).

There are several reasons why SMEs prefer to offer informal, *ad hoc* training to their employees, beyond cost considerations. Curran et al. (1997) supports the argument that SME employers prefer informal training and development for ensuring employees have up-to-date skills. The typical training approach in these firms is through direct supervision or coaching by an experienced employee or manager, except in roles where accredited skills are required. Another reason is related to the disruption that comes with employees having to leave work to attend external training (Keep, 2006). The cost involved in training employees in smaller organisations is much greater than in large organisations due to economies of scale. There is also a fear that employees may leave the organisation for higher paid opportunities after gaining desirable training. While this may happen in large organisations also, the impact is greater in small organisations that do not have contingencies for this type of scenarios.

Although training may take place on an *ad hoc* basis in smaller firms, it is hard to quantify how much of it is taking place (Curran et al., 1997).

Research by Barrett (2015) found that owner/manager attitudes in small firms influenced decisions around training, although they were not independent of the regulatory framework or the economic and social conditions within which the firm operated. Where small firms engaged in training, this was job-related and non-strategic, occurring on a day-to-day basis. Other, less frequently used methods include external training courses during work time, induction training and internal off-the-job training courses (Jameson, 2000).

In terms of management development, softer management skills, such as financial, marketing, HR, strategy, planning and operations management, can enable small firms to grow (Fuller-Love, 2006). However, management development initiatives have been found to be underutilised too due to financial and resource constraints, including the lack of qualified senior managers (Smith and Whittaker, 1999) or the lack of management training of owners (Fuller-Love, 2006).

Bearing in mind the earlier discussion about the SME approach to training and development, Macpherson and Jayawarna (2007) argue that firm circumstances moderate this approach. They identify a number of influential factors, such as specific firm characteristics (e.g. size, years of operation, ownership), product factors and market conditions (e.g. technology), and the way responsibilities and management roles are assigned (e.g. organisational structures). For example, organisational size affects the number of specialist posts in the firm, and therefore, the need to develop new skills through training and development. Size also affects the formalisation of HRM practices (Krishnan and Scullion, 2017) and the development of an HR function that would be responsible for pursuing a training and development strategy (Fabi et al., 2009). Similarly, a firm that is manufacturing innovative products may invest more in training and development (Macpherson and Jayawarna, 2007). Ownership of the firm is another determining factor; for example, family businesses have been found to be primarily reactive rather than proactive, while training and development is predominantly viewed as individual career development not adding much to the business (Macpherson and Jayawarna, 2007). As family businesses experience growth, they may start to utilise training and development practices, but the formalisation of these practices is unlikely (Birdthistle, 2006).

Employee Relations

SMEs generally compare poorly with larger firms in relation to salaries, fringe benefits, holiday entitlements, training opportunities, working hours and labour turnover (European Foundation, 2001). Health and safety is a particular concern in sectors such as agriculture, manufacturing, construction and transport, where employees are also more likely to suffer accidents and to be exposed to hazards (Holten and Crouch, 2014).

Research has also found a high level of ignorance from both employers and employees in relation to employment legislation (MacMahon, 1996), and this may explain, to some extent, why SMEs compare poorly in working conditions in relation to larger firms.

A range of factors affect the level of formalisation of voice channels in SMEs (Sameer and Ozbilgin, 2014). On the one hand, employees in small enterprises are seen as rather quiescent, not engaging in overt conflict with management (Wilkinson et al., 2007). On the other hand, managers engage more in information than consultation because they see the latter as a threat to management control (Dundon and Gollan, 2007) and are less likely to have formally approved information and consultation agreements (Wilkinson et al., 2007). This means that union membership and collective bargaining coverage are weak in SMEs, although they are not entirely non-existent (Holten and Crouch, 2014). The incidence of social dialogue and employee representation in general is lower than in larger firms (Eurofound, 2011). For example, according to Eurofound (2011), union membership in EU SMEs tends to rise with increasing company size. Very small firms that are usually family-run do not have a culture of collective employee representation involving trade unions. Research by Holten and Crouch (2014) found that the owner's negative perception of unions may pose a significant role conflict for employees who are union members, which may, in turn, discourage employees from union membership, thereby creating a culture of non-membership. In addition, collective representation is not obligatory for small firms in many countries. The sector also plays a role in union density, with companies in the public sector more likely to be unionised than those in the private sector. Where employee representation at company level exists, this exhibits great variation in form across different institutional settings, ranging from health and safety committees or representatives, trade unions and works councils (Eurofound, 2011).

In the case of non-unionised SMEs, employee relations take the form of direct and informal voice channels between employer and employee (Marlow and Gray, 2005). However, Barry and Wilkinson (2016: 265) argue that 'setting up employee voice mechanisms potentially allows staff to influence events at work, but having a voice does not mean it is listened to', and this highlights the fact that even if SMEs have voice channels present, they may not be used effectively. Informal voice is also affected by the macroeconomic context, such as the recent financial crisis, which makes employees in SMEs afraid or unwilling to speak up about organisational issues that concern them (Prouska and Psychogios, 2016; Prouska and Psychogios, 2018). In addition, the breadth and depth of voice is affected by the owner's ability to reconcile issues of power and control (Gilman et al., 2015); when owner-managers struggle with the changing nature of control, voice remains shallow, adolescent and informal, while when owner-managers embrace internal challenges, they champion formal voice mechanisms.

Performance and Reward Management

The purpose of performance management is to encourage employees to take responsibility for their skills and contribution to firm performance. Around one-fifth of SMEs employ a range of performance management procedures, which include recognising unions, work arrangement flexibility, equal opportunity employment practices and pay for performance schemes (Forth et al., 2006). Nevertheless, as in other HR practices, performance management and appraisals seem to be more informal rather than formal. However, there is some evidence suggesting that there is a positive experience of applying performance management systems in SMEs. For example, Tennant and Tanoren (2005) suggest that smaller firms can implement the balance scorecard approach in order to experience improved performance and productivity.

A study by Hudson et al. (2001) provided an extensive literature review on approaches to performance measurement practices in SMEs. According to this study, an effective performance measurement system should be developed upon three aspects: the requirements of the process, the characteristics of the performance measures and the dimensions of performance. Comparing this typology with their practical findings in SMEs, they concluded that there are numerous insufficiencies related to various factors, the most important ones referring to non-compliance with a company's strategy and goals, great emphasis only on financial performance, insistence on indicators that are not of real use or too complex or impractical, lack of useful feedback exploitation and exclusion of a multidimensional approach to performance. In a similar vein, Garengo et al. (2005) reviewed the literature and analysed the characteristics and determinants of performance management in SMEs. They argued that SMEs face five challenges in applying performance management: (1) inability to complete the process due to lack of time for non-operational activities and the low commitment of higher management; (2) incorrect adaptation of systems that work well for big-scale companies with the notion of '*making small what was big*'; (3) lack of a holistic approach in all operations but only to the financial ones; (4) inadequate planning with a reactive (non-proactive) mentality; and (5) restricted availability of resources for extended data processes. In addition, Garengo and Bernardi (2007) support that performance management systems are a great means of growth and development for SMEs. They also suggest that there are four main aspects affecting the implementation of a performance management system in SMEs, namely the governance structure, the business model, the information management systems combined with the employee behaviour, and the management style applied. The importance of a performance management system, as a strategic tool, declines when the governance of the company passes from managers and external shareholders to owners. Moreover, a change in the existing business model triggers the interest in applications in the field of performance management. In a similar vein, a recent study by Garengo and Sharma (2014) supported that applying a performance management tool in SMEs requires change in corporate governance.

In terms of how rewards are overall applied in SMEs, there is the perception that larger SMEs provide more rewards than smaller firms (Mayson and Barret, 2006). However, rewards vary between different SME sectors (Harney and Dundon, 2006). Research has found that SMEs who are part of a franchise and those that are unionised adopt more sophisticated reward management systems, including implementing a total rewards approach (Urbano and Yordanova, 2008). Specifically in terms of total rewards, SMEs are more likely to adopt such an approach if they are actively promoting close and harmonious relationships among employees and therefore invest in providing a good work environment (Wilkinson, 1999). On the contrary, SMEs not promoting employee autonomy or involvement and characterised by poorer working conditions and are less likely to adopt any aspects of a total rewards approach (Cunningham, 2010).

However, we cannot easily generalise the approach SMEs take in reward management. Research suggests that the institutional context plays a critical role in the formulation of reward strategies in SMEs. For example, in transitioning economies, because there is a low level of unionisation among SMEs, the adoption of HR practices including total rewards is often minimal or non-existent (Prouska et al., 2016; Welte and David, 2009). Similarly, Tonoyan et al. (2010) found that the lack of employment law enforcement in transitioning economies makes SMEs more likely to ignore employment policies and practices, including those relating to pay and compensation. This is in contrast to SMEs in Australia, for example, where reward management strategies are more widely used (Wiesner, 2010).

Where reward strategies are less developed, performance management practices are informal and applied on an *ad hoc* basis (Wilkinson, 1999). When SMEs pay for performance, this is in addition to basic pay (Zhend et al., 2007). Appraisal systems are generic; they tend to be simpler and directly managed by the owners of the company. This reflects the informality within SMEs as a main contextual factor. Although SMEs apply more informal and *ad hoc* methods of appraising employees (Wilkinson, 1999), they tend to be more constructive because feedback and development can be given instantly and easily (MacMahon and Murphy, 1999). However, performance management systems in SMEs are used to provide performance feedback to employees and are not linked to a reward system of bonuses (Prouska et al., 2016).

Summary

Chapter 2 explored the SME approach to HRM and provided an over-view of how SMEs apply core HR practices. The chapter discussed that SMEs implement informal, emergent and reactive management practices, including HRM practices. HRM in SMEs is usually performed by the owner or senior manager. SMEs usually do not have internal HR expertise or skills, but as organisational size increases, HR policies and practices become more formalised and the presence of an HR department is more likely. Within this informal setting, this chapter has explored a range of HRM practices in SMEs, such as talent management, resourcing, training and development, employee relations, performance and rewards management. The remaining chapters of this book explore HRM in SMEs in a variety of diverse regions.

References

Arthur, D. (1995). *Managing Human Resources in Small and Mid-sized Companies*. New York: American Association of Management.

Atkinson, J. and Meager, N. (1994). Running to stand still: The small firm in the labour market. In J. Atkinson and D. Storey, eds., *Employment, the Small Firm and the Labour Market*. London: Routledge.

Bacon, N. and Hoque, K. (2005). HRM in the SME sector: Valuable employees and coercive networks. *The International Journal of Human Resource Management*, 16(11): pp. 1976–1999.

Bacon, N., Storey, J., Ackers, P. and Coates, D. (1996). It's a small world: Managing human resources in small businesses. *The International Journal of Human Resource Management*, 7: pp. 82–100.

Barney, J. (1991). Firm resources and sustained competitive advantage. *Journal of Management*, 17(1): pp. 99–120.

Barrett, R. (2015). Small firm training: Just meeting the day-to-day needs of the business. *Employee Relations*, 37(5): pp. 547–567.

Barrett, R. and Mayson, S. (2007). Human resource management in growing small firms. *Journal of Small Business and Enterprise Development*, 14(2): pp.307–320.

Barrett, R., Neeson, R. and Billington, L. (2007). Finding the 'right staff' in small firms. *Education and Training*, 49(8/9): pp. 686–697.

Barry, M. and Wilkinson, A. (2016). Pro-social or pro-management? A critique of the conception of employee voice within organisational behaviour. *British Journal of Industrial Relations*, 54(2): pp. 261–284.

Bartram, T. (2005). Small firms, big ideas: The adoption of human resource management in Australian small firms. *Asia Pacific Review*, 43(1): pp. 137–154.

Behrends, T. (2007). Recruitment practices in small and medium size enterprises: An empirical study among knowledge-intensive professional service firms. *Management Review*, 18(1): pp. 55–74.

Billett, S., Hernon-Tinning, B. and Ehrich, L. (2003). Small business pedagogic practices. *Journal of Vocational Education and Training*, 55(2): pp. 149–167.

Birdthistle, N. (2006). Training and learning strategies of family businesses: An Irish case. *Journal of European Industrial Training*, 30(7): pp. 550–568.

Budhwar, P. S. and Debrah, Y. (2001). Rethinking comparative and cross-national human resource management research. *The International Journal of Human Resource Management*, 12(3): pp. 497–515.

Cameron, L., Miller, P. and Frew, E. (2010). Relationship marketing in the recruitment and retention of service industry staff in family-owned businesses. *Journal of Human Resources in Hospitality and Tourism*, 9(1): pp. 71–91.

Cardon, M. S. and Stevens, C. E. (2004). Managing human resources in small organisations: What do we know? *Human Resource Management Review*, 14(3): pp. 295–323.

Carroll, M., Marchington, M., Earnshaw, J. and Taylor, S. (1999). Recruitment in small firms: Processes, methods and problems. *Employee Relations*, 21(3): pp. 236–250.

Cassell, C., Nadin, S., Gray, M. and Clegg, C. (2002). Exploring human resource management practices in small and medium sized enterprises. *Personnel Review*, 31(6): pp. 671–692.

Cui, W., Khan, Z. and Tarba, S. Y. (2018). Strategic talent management in service SMEs of China. *Thunderbird International Business Review*, 60(1): pp. 9–20.

Cunningham, L. X. (2010). Managing human resources in SMEs in a transition economy: Evidence from China. *The International Journal of Human Resource Management*, 21(12): pp. 2120–2141.

Curran, J., Blackburn, R., Kitchins, J. and Worth, J. (1997). Small firms and workforce training: Some results, analysis and policy implications from a national survey. In M. Ram, D. Deakins and D. Smallbone, eds., *Small Firms: Enterprising Futures*. London: Paul Chapman, pp. 90–101.

De Kok, J. and Uhlaner, L. M. (2001). Organisational context and human resource management in the small firm. *Small Business Economic*, 17(4): pp. 273–291.

Dietz, G., Wiele, T., Iwaarden, J. and Brosseau, J. (2006). HRM inside UK e-commerce firms. *International Small Business Journal*, 24(5): pp. 443–470.

Dundon, T. and Gollan, P. (2007). Re-conceptualising non-union voice. *The International Journal of Human Resource Management*, 18(7): pp. 1182–1198.

Edwards, P. and Ram, M. (2009). HRM in small firms: Respecting and regulating informality. In A. Wilkinson, N. Bacon, T. Redman and S. Snell, eds., *The Sage Handbook of Human Resource Management*. London: Sage.

Eurofound (2011). *SMEs in the crisis: Employment, industrial relations and local partnership*. [online]. Available at: www.eurofound.europa.eu/observatories/ eurwork/comparative-information/smes-in-the-crisis-employment-industrial-relations-and-local-partnership. [Accessed 20 December 2017].

European Commission (2017). *Annual Report on European SMEs 2016/17*. European Union: European Commission.

European Foundation (2001). *Employment Relations in Micro and Small Enterprises in the EU: Literature Review*. Dublin: European Foundation.

Fabi, B., Raymond, L. and Lacoursière, R. (2009). Strategic alignment of HRM practices in manufacturing SMEs: A Gestalts perspective. *Journal of Small Business and Enterprise Development*, 16(1): pp. 7–25.

Festing, M., Schäfer, L. and Scullion, H. (2013). Talent management in medium-sized German companies: An explorative study and agenda for future research. *The International Journal of Human Resource Management*, 24(9): pp. 1872–1893.

Forth, J., Bewley, H. and Bryson, A. (2006). *Small and Medium-sized Enterprises: Findings from the 2004 Workplace Employee Relations Survey*. London: Department of Trade and industry.

Fuller-Love, N. (2006). Management development in small firms. *International Journal of Management Reviews*, 8(3): pp. 175–190.

Galanaki, E. and Papalexandris, N. (2005). Outsourcing of human resource management services in Greece. *International Journal of Manpower*, 26(4): pp. 382–396.

Garengo, P. and Bernardi, G. (2007). Organisational capability in SMEs: Performance measurement as a key system in supporting company development. *International Journal of Productivity and Performance Management*, 56(5/6): pp. 518–532.

Garengo, P., Biazzo, S. and Bititci, U. S. (2005). Performance measurement systems in SMEs: A review for a research agenda. *International journal of management reviews*, 7(1): pp. 25–47.

Garengo, P. and Sharma, M. K. (2014). Performance measurement system contingency factors: A cross analysis of Italian and Indian SMEs. *Production Planning and Control*, 25(3): pp. 220–240.

Gilman, M., Raby, S. and Pyman, A. (2015). The contours of employee voice in SMEs: The importance of context. *Human Resource Management Journal*, 25(4): pp. 563–579.

Hanks, S. H. and Chandler, G. N. (1994). Patterns of functional specialisation in emerging high-tech firms. *Journal of Small Business Management*, 32(2): pp. 22–37.

Harney, B. and Dundon, T. (2006). Capturing complexity: Developing an integrated approach to analysing HRM in SMEs. *Human Resource Management Journal*, 16(1): pp. 48–73.

Hodgkinson, G. P., Langan-Fox, J. and Sadler-Smith, E. (2008). Intuition: A fundamental bridging construct in the behavioural sciences. *British Journal of Psychology*, 99: pp. 1–27.

Holten, A. L. and Crouch, C. (2014). Unions in small and medium-sized enterprises: A family factor perspective. *European Journal of Industrial Relations*, 20(3): pp. 273–290.

Hudson, M., Smart, A. and Bourne, M. (2001). Theory and practice in SME performance measurement systems. *International journal of operations and production management*, 21(8): pp. 1096–1115.

Hunt, K. G. (2017). Cultivate talent by cultivating culture. *Journal of Property Management*, 82(4): pp. 8–11.

Jameson, S. M. (2000). Recruitment and training in small firms. *Journal of European Industrial Training*, 24(1): pp. 43–49.

Jones, J. T. (2010). Pedagogic practices associates with management development: A study of growing small firms. *The International Journal of Learning*, 17(1): pp. 309–318.

Kaliannan, M., Abraham, M. and Ponnusamy, V. (2016). Effective talent management in Malaysian SMEs: A proposed framework. *The Journal of Developing Areas*, 50(5): pp. 393–401.

Keep, E. (2006). Market failure in skills. *SSDA Catalyst*, 1: pp. 1–9.

Kerr, G., Way, S. A. and Thacker, J. (2007). Performance, HR practices and the HR manager in small entrepreneurial firms. *Journal of Small Business and Entrepreneurship*, 20(1): pp. 55–68.

Kontoghiorghes, C. (2016). Linking high performance organisational culture and talent management: Satisfaction/motivation and organisational commitment as mediators. *International Journal of Human Resource Management*, 27(16): pp. 1833–1853.

Kotey, B. and Slade, P. (2005). Formal human resource management practices in small growing firms. *Journal of Small Business Management*, 43(1): pp. 16–40.

Krishnan, T. N. and Scullion, H. (2017). Talent management and dynamic view of talent in small and medium enterprises. *Human Resource Management Review*, 27(3): pp. 431–441.

Kroon, B., Voorde, K. and Timmers, J. (2013). High performance work practices in small firms: A resource-poverty and strategic decision-making perspective. *Small Business Economics*, 41(1): pp. 71–91.

Leung, A. (2003). Different ties for different needs: Recruitment practices of entrepreneurial firms at different developmental phases. *Human Resource Management*, 42(4): pp. 303–320.

Litz, R. A. and Stewart, A. C. (2000). Research note: Trade name franchise membership as a human resource management strategy: Does buying group training deliver 'true value' for small retailers? *Entrepreneurship: Theory and Practice*, 25: pp. 125–125.

Lodato, M. A. (2008). *Going with Your Gut: An Investigation of Why Managers Prefer Intuitive Employee Selection*. Ohio: Bowling Green State University.

MacMahon, J. (1996). Employee relations in small firms in Ireland: An exploratory study of small manufacturing firms. *Employee Relations*, 18(5): pp. 66–80.

MacMahon, J. and Murphy, E. (1999). Managerial effectiveness in small enterprises: Implications for HRD. *Journal of European Industrial Training*, 23(1): pp.25–35.

Macpherson, A. and Jayawarna, D. (2007). Training approaches in manufacturing SMEs: Measuring the influence of ownership, structure and markets. *Education and Training*, 49(8/9): pp. 698–719.

Marlow, S. (2000). Investigating the use of emergent strategic human resource management activity in the small firm. *Journal of Small Business and Enterprise Development*, 7(2): pp. 135–148.

Marlow, S. (2002). Regulating labour management in small firms. *Human Resource Management Journal*, 12(3): pp. 25–43.

Marlow, S. and Gray, C. (2005). Information and consultation in small and medium-sized enterprises. In J. Storey, ed., *Adding Value through Information and Consultation*. Basingstoke: Palgrave Macmillan, pp. 21–28.

Marlow, S. and Patton, D. (2002). Minding the gap between employers and employees: The challenge for owner-managers or smaller manufacturing firms. *Employee Relations*, 24(5): pp. 523–539.

Mayer-Haug, K., Read, S., Brinckmann, J., Dew, N. and Grichnik, D. (2013). Entrepreneurial talent and venture performance: A meta-analytic investigation of SMEs. *Research Policy*, 42(6–7): pp. 1251–1273.

Mayson, S. and Barrett, R. (2006). The 'science' and 'practice' of HRM in small firms. *Human Resource Management Review*, 16(4): pp. 447–455.

Meutia, T. I. and Bukhori, A. (2017). The role of feedback and feed forward control system to improve competitive advantage of SMEs in Indonesia. *European Research Studies*, 20(2): pp. 496–506.

Nguyen, T. and Bryant, S. (2004). A study of the formality of human resource management practices in small and medium-size enterprises in Vietnam. *International Small Business Journal*, 22(6): pp. 595–618.

Prouska, R. and Psychogios, A. G. (2016). Do not say a word! Conceptualising employee silence in a long-term crisis context. *The International Journal of Human Resource Management*, 29(5): pp. 885–914.

Prouska, R. and Psychogios, A. G. (2018). Should I say something? A framework for understanding silence from a line manager's perspective during an economic crisis. *Economic and Industrial Democracy*. doi:10.1177/0143831X17752869.

Prouska, R., Psychogios, A. G. and Rexhepi, Y. (2016). Rewarding employees in turbulent economies for improved organisational performance: Exploring SMEs in the South-Eastern European region. *Personnel Review*, 45(6): pp. 1259–1280.

Psychogios, A. G., Szamosi, T. L., Prouska, R. and Brewster, C. (2016). A three-fold framework for understanding HRM practices in south-eastern European SMEs. *Employee Relations*, 38(3): pp. 310–331.

Rainnie, A. (1989). *Industrial Relations in Small Firms*. London: Routledge.

Sameer, M. and Ozbilgin, M. F. (2014). Employee voice in the SME context. In A. Wilkinson, J. Donaghey, T. Dundon and B. Freeman, eds., *Handbook of Research on Employee Voice*. Cheltenham: Edward Elgar Publishing, pp. 410–420.

Sharmila, A. and Gopalakrishnan, K. (2013). An implementation of talent management on SMEs. *Global Management Review*, 7(2): pp. 40–43.

Singh, M. and Vohra, N. (2009). Level of formalisation of human resource management in small and medium enterprises in India. *Journal of Entrepreneurship*, 18(1): pp. 95–116.

Sisson, K. (1993). In search of human resource management. *British Journal of Industrial Relations*, 31(2): pp. 201–210.

Smith, A. and Whittaker, J. (1999). Management development in SMEs: What needs to be done? *Journal of Small Business and Enterprise Development*, 5(2): pp. 176–185.

Stahl, G. K., Bjorkman, I., Farndale, E., Morris, S. S., Paauwe, J., Stiles, P. and Wright, P. (2012). Six principles of effective global talent management. *MIT Sloan Management Review*, 53(2): pp. 25–32.

Stavrou-Costea, E. and Manson, B. (2006). HRM in small and medium enterprises: Typical, but typically ignored. In: H. H. Larsen and W. Mayrhofer, eds., *Managing Human Resources in Europe*. London: Routledge, pp. 107–130.

Stonehouse, G. and Pemberton, J. (2002). Strategic planning in SMEs – Some Empirical Findings. *Management Decision*, 40(9): pp. 853–861.

Storey, D. J. (1994). *Understanding the Small Business Sector*. New York: Routledge.

Storey, D. J., Saridakis, G., Sen-Gupta, S., Edwards, P. K. and Blackburn, R. A. (2010). Linking HR formality with employee job quality: The role of firm and workplace size. *Human Resource Management*, 49(2): pp. 305–329.

Tatoglu, E., Glaister, A. J. and Demirbag, M. (2016). Talent management motives and practices in an emerging market: A comparison between MNEs and local firms. *Journal of World Business*, 51(2): pp. 278–293.

Taylor, S. (2010). The hunting of the snark. In S. Malow, D. Patton and M. Ram, eds., *Labour Management in Small Firms*. London: Routledge, pp. 18–42.

Tennant, C. and Tanoren, M. (2005). Performance management in SMEs: A balanced scorecard perspective. *International Journal of Business Performance Management*, 7: pp. 123–143.

Tonoyan, V., Strohmejer, R., Habib, M. and Perlitz, M. (2010). Corruption and entrepreneurship: How formal and informal institutions shape small firm behaviour in transitioning and mature market economies. *Entrepreneurship Theory and Practice*, 34(5): pp. 803–831.

Tsai, C., Sen Gupta, S. and Edwards, P. (2007). When and why is small beautiful? The experience of work in the small firm. *Human Relations*, 60(12): pp. 1779–1807.

Tyagarajan, N. (2013). The great global talent hunt. *Financial Executive*, 29(6): pp. 48–50.

Urbano, D. and Yordanova, D. (2008). Determinants of the adoption of HRM practices in tourism SMEs in Spain. *Business and Economics*, 2(3): pp. 167–185.

Valverde, M., Scullion, H. and Ryan, G. (2013). Talent management in Spanish medium-sized organisations. *The International Journal of Human Resource Management*, 24(9): pp. 1832–1852.

Welte, F. and David, S. (2009). *Handbook of Research on Entrepreneurship Policies in Central and Eastern Europe*. Northampton: Edward Elgar.

Westhead, P. and Storey, D. (1996). Management training and small firm performance: Why is the link so weak? *International Small Business Journal*, 14(4): pp. 13–24.

Wiesner, R. (2010). Bleak house or bright prospect? HRM in Australian SMEs over 1998–2008. *Asia Pacific Journal of Human Resources*, 48(2): pp. 151–184.

Wilkinson, A. (1999). Employment relations in SMEs. *Employee Relations*, 22(3): pp. 206–217.

Wilkinson, A., Dundon, T. and Grugulis, I. (2007). Information but not consultation: Exploring employee involvement in SMEs. *The International Journal of Human Resource Management*, 18(7): pp. 1279–1297.

Williamson, I. O., Cable, D. M. and Aldrich, H. E. (2002). Smaller but not necessarily weaker: how small businesses can overcome barriers to recruitment. In J. Katz and T. M. Welbourne, eds., *Managing People in Entrepreneurial Organisations: Learning from the Merger of Entrepreneurship and Human Resource Management*. Amsterdam: Jai Press, pp. 83–106.

Zhend, C., O'Neil, G. and Morrison, M. (2007). Ownership and strategic choice of HRM methods by Chinese SMEs. *Asia Pacific Journal of Economics and Business*, 11(1): pp. 25–39.

3   HRM in SMEs in Emerging Market Economies I – Asia and the Pacific

Introduction

EMEs have become extremely attractive in the last decade or so, not only to researchers and business management scholars but also to various practitioners, investors and organisations from both the private and public sectors. The term first appeared in 1981 by the economist Antoine Van Agtmael, and it refers to a business phenomenon that is not fully described by or constrained to geography or economic strength (Cox, 2017). According to Kvint (2009), an EME is a society in transitioning from a dictatorship to a free market-oriented economy, with increasing economic freedom, gradual integration with the global marketplace and with other members of the global emerging market, an expanding middle class, improving standards of living, social stability and tolerance, as well as an increase in cooperation with multilateral institutions. However, not all EME can be classified as 'dictatorships' before their transformation process to more liberal markets has started. Therefore, the aforementioned definition does not cover all the aforementioned countries, but focuses mainly on some of them. In this respect, the Emerging Economy Report (2008) defines EMEs as those regions of the world that are experiencing rapid informationalisation under conditions of limited or partial industrialisation. Once more, this definition emphasises one aspect of EMEs while neglecting other aspects. For example, Marois (2012) argues that EMEs are related, among other things, to the development of the idea of 'emerging finance capitalism' – an era wherein the collective interests of financial capital principally shape the logical options and choices of government and state elites over and above those of labour and popular classes.

For the purpose of this book, we adopt a more generic but at the same time holistic definition of the term that can help us better comprehend HRM in SMEs in these markets. This definition is provided by the Financial Dictionary (2018), according to which an EME refers to a country's economy that is progressing towards becoming more advanced, usually by means of rapid growth and industrialisation. These countries experience an expanding role both in the world economy and on the political frontier. We would add to this definition that the transformation process refers to the society of these countries, and it follows a liberalisation approach although maintaining specific logics, like informality. For example, some aspects of EMEs include increased market orientation, low income, rapid growth and expansion of economic foundation but also a considerable size informal economy (Williams, 2014; Williams and Nadin, 2010). Such countries are considered to be in the process of changing status from developing to developed and include many countries in Africa, most countries in Eastern and South-Eastern Europe,[1] some countries of Latin America, some countries in the Middle East, and some countries in Asia and South East Asia. The success of these economies is important, because they are rapidly becoming key economic forces in the world (Bruton et al., 2008). It is estimated that approximately 80% of the world's population live in EMEs representing about 20% of the world's economies (Heakal, 2017).

It is worth mentioning that EMEs are not homogenous (Tung and Aycan, 2008). There are some basic similarities, mainly related to the historical development of the political, social and economic context of the majority of these countries (Aycan, 2004; Punnett, 2004). For example, many of these countries are heavily reliant on agricultural production, while they have less developed institutions and great inequalities in terms of access to higher education as well as to funding opportunities. At the same time, EMEs have major differences. For instance, there are salient societal as well as cultural differences between EMEs in Asia and those in Central and Eastern Europe (Tung and Aycan, 2008). In this respect, this chapter focuses on EMEs in Asia and the Pacific, particularly on the role of SMEs and HRM in this context. The following two chapters explore EMEs in Africa (Chapter 4) and Latin America (Chapter 5).

HRM in Emerging Markets

There is a growing interest in EMEs in the management literature (Wright et al., 2005a). However, we have less knowledge of management practices applied by SMEs in these types of economies (Bruton et al., 2008). HRM in SMEs in emerging markets is 'under reconstruction', meaning that it is passing through transition (Cooke et al., 2011). This transition phase is influenced by historical, cultural as well as institutional aspects which can determine the way specific management practices, including

---

1 In this book, we approach and examine countries in Eastern and South-Eastern Europe (mainly post-communist) as economies in transition, although the term can be equated with the term EMEs. The reason is that these countries followed a similar political transformation and economic liberalisation process in comparison with other emerging economies in Asia, Africa and Latin America.

HR, are adopted by various (small and large) organisations in EMEs (Yan, 2003). However, there is evidence suggesting that the level of SME integration, especially of SME internationalisation in these countries, increases with modernisation and adoption of HR management practices (Psychogios et al., 2016). For example, a study by Khavul et al. (2010) found that when SMEs internationalise, either into more economically developed countries or into countries with stronger employment regulations, they also invest more in HRM practices. Still, though, the evidence around the use of HRM practices in SMEs in EMEs is limited. In this respect, this section seeks to understand and explore the aspects that influence the application of HR practices in specific EMEs. Although there is no intention to offer a cross-cultural or cross-national comparison of HRM in SMEs in EMEs, this chapter and the next two chapters review the current state of knowledge for specific countries in three regions: Asia and the Pacific (Chapter 3), Africa (Chapter 4) and Latin America (Chapter 5).

HRM in SMEs in Asia and the Pacific

China

The People's Republic of China is presently the fourth largest economy in the world and projected to become the second largest by 2030 (Au et al., 2008). Its main growth engine has been the private sector, which runs on market capitalist principles of profits-driven private equity and ownership, alongside the state sector, predicated on socialist centralised command economy principles (Au et al., 2008). China is in the process of transforming itself to a market-oriented economy. In this sense, it is not surprising that private companies are expanding quickly. Private companies gained the support and investment from government gradually. However, most of them are SMEs. SMEs, notably those operating in the informal sector, constitute the vast majority of businesses. In 2015, SMEs made up about 97.9% of all registered companies in China and contributed to 58% of the GDP and 68% of exports (Hoffmann, 2017).

The expansion of private companies was the response to a series of economic and social issues in China, such as unemployment. The blooming of private companies creates value, which, in turn, pushes the economic growth further. That is to say, the process of being a 'well off society' is accelerated. With the continued growth and expansion of private companies, especially SMEs, owners and managers must increase the number of workers and strengthen HRM and HR operations so that they can keep businesses and enterprises running (Mazzarol, 2003).

However, it seems that there are some issues regarding the HRM function in Chinese SMEs. For example, it is difficult to gain and preserve high-quality employees (Mazzarol, 2003). It seems that many Chinese SMEs focus on low-level employees since the labour cost is less. According to Cappelli (2008), lower-level jobs may be easily and cheaply filled by outsiders, because the required competencies are readily available, making the costs of undershooting demand relatively modest. For more highly skilled jobs, the costs of undershooting are much higher as compared to the former.

As qualified and highly qualified HR supply in the labour market is limited, training and professional development for staff (especially low-level) becomes a key challenge for Chinese SMEs (Zheng et al., 2009). Training is one of the key HRM practices in SMEs and an inevitable requirement for developing the competence of a workforce so that they can work with new methods and technologies in the new and changing environment (Child, 1991). However, employee training in Chinese small companies is a major issue. In China, there is a tradition of training from childhood to rely on superiors and the group for guidance in dealing with the unexpected. This makes Chinese less capable of flexibility, problem-solving and taking individual responsibility (Bond, 1996), all of which are considered core skills for long-term development in companies (Wright et al., 2005b).

Similar to training and development of employees in Chinese SMEs, talent management also poses challenges for these firms. Gao and Banerji (2015) explain that in China, many talented SME employees consider smaller companies as a stepping stone for moving to large corporations. This means a constant loss of highly skilled employees that SMEs cannot retain. Moreover, Cui et al. (2018) argue that in SMEs in China, managers usually do not distinguish HR policies from talent management policies due to lack of knowledge. However, there is some evidence of talent management practices applied. For example, many SME managers emphasise that a good company reputation, as well as a strong brand image, can attract talent. According to the same study, these factors can work better at attracting talent than a friendly and reward-oriented working environment. In the same study, Cui et al. (2018) state that Chinese managers in SMEs consider 'talent' as having the right person at the right job. In this direction, when it comes to recruitment of talents, their study shows that SME managers use internships as a talent attraction tool. In a similar vein, Tyagarajan (2013) explains that China can show growth rates only in terms of developing highly capable and skilled workers. In this respect, SMEs, by cooperating with large companies, can develop better capabilities in managing talent.

Furthermore, most Chinese SMEs recruit and select new employees on criteria that many times go beyond the typical methods of this HR practice. For instance, while most managers consider job interviews as a crucial step in recruiting key personnel, they are still less favoured in the selection process in Chinese firms (Zhu and Dowling, 2002). In a similar vein, other selection methods, such as psychometric tests, assessment centres and so on, have a limited place in the Chinese SME industry (Verburg, 1996). Ko and Liu (2017) indicate that SMEs primarily use their contacts through family, friends and networks to fill posts. Huo and Von Glinow (1995) argued that the major reason behind this approach is that observing personality and interpersonal skills, a key purpose of recruitment interviews, seems to not be appreciated in the Chinese cultural context. However, there is a trend, although limited, of Chinese SMEs adopting more transparent and sophisticated recruitment procedures in recent years (Cooke, 2005).

Another noticeable aspect of Chinese enterprises is the importance of connection in selection practices, well known as 'Guanxi' (Liu et al., 2016). 'Guanxi' is not a one-dimensional concept but a group of concepts that describe how individuals connect and should behave in relationships, such as 'mianzi' (face), 'jia-ren' (family members), 'renqing' (a debt to an acquaintance) and 'guanxi-hu' (specially connected individuals) (Ko and Liu, 2017). Traditionally, the importance of connections is reflected in the political and social systems, which have been geared to numerous types of affiliation, such as family, clan or kinship. The strong sense of close personal relationship and obligation that is nurtured in the early stages of recruitment becomes one of the major impediments in the firing process, as managers tend to be highly protective of their employees so as to maintain staff loyalty (Child, 1991). Chinese culture can be a possible explanation of the HRM approach in SMEs since it is characterised by a spirit of compromise and tolerance, while most of the HR practices that have been developed and applied in a Western cultural context are based on formal and fully professional working practices (Wood et al., 2007). This approach to HRM can also be explained by the nature of Chinese institutions, particularly the education system, which encourages students to be patient, understanding and considerate at different stages of their education (Bond, 1996). The education system is a strong institution in China, as it provides a far more reliable means by which Chinese SMEs can select an employee and, in a sense, rely on his/her future success (Huo and Von Glinow, 1995).

Moreover, Chinese culture enhances collective actions. In this respect, collective decision-making and shared responsibility are being widely used and have being encouraged in China. Zheng et al. (2009) observe that the majority of SMEs in China have adopted team-based decision-making and information-sharing processes and practices to encourage and motivate employees to take part in decision-making, aiming at increasing performance. Nevertheless, the way in which SMEs encourage employee participation in decision-making has not been well-documented (Zheng et al., 2009). Collective decision-making is also limited to operational issues, while strategic decision-making is controlled by owners and managers (Hamel, 2009).

In addition, employee involvement is generally problematic in Chinese SMEs. The importance of employee involvement is that it is an attempt to create a sense of belonging and commitment via the dissemination of information about the organisation and its environment (Rowley and Benson, 2003). This is less likely among Chinese SMEs, since Chinese culture creates obstacles to effective communication, discouraging, in most cases, employee involvement. Similarly, the importance of family in society has encouraged managers and employers to enhance hierarchical control and obedience in order to strengthen their own authority (Whitley, 1992).

Hofstede (1980) states that Chinese society emphasises a collective orientation and encourages shared responsibility and social interests. This has a clear impact on reward policies in Chinese SMEs. As Wilhelm and Xia (1993) claim, people in China do not thrive on public praise from others and would never praise themselves while in a group situation. They do not try to acquire prestige by making social change. In addition, there is often a lingering caution in the enterprises about allowing wage differentials among the workforce to widen too much (Tang and Ward, 2003). For instance, Chinese SME managers are unwilling to poorly rate their subordinates, since this would negatively affect their personal relationships at work (Bjorkman and Fan, 2002). Easterby-Smith et al. (1995) proclaim that the main difference between HR practices in China and other developed countries appears in the softer areas where relationships are important, such as rewards. Moreover, Bjorkman and Fan (2002) point out that a common problem in reward systems is lack of employee initiative and the taking on of responsibility by employees, which is likely to be rooted both in Chinese culture and in the institutional context of Chinese SMEs.

In summary, Chinese HRM and employment practices in SMEs are without a doubt culturally and institutionally bound. However, there are some indications that Chinese SMEs have started to modernise themselves, particularly due to a great internationalisation process that brought clients and collaborators from other countries. This trend has enabled SMEs to become more open to the adoption of more formalised and sophisticated HR practices. These strong cultural forces can prove a critical factor in the process of adopting HR practices in future.

India

The Indian economy is now the second fastest growing economy of the world. As per the Ministry of Finance, India's GDP growth in 2017 was 6.7% compared to the previous year, with a projection for its GDP to grow by 8.15% in 2022. In such a visible growth environment, tremendous efforts are being made by SMEs to make their prominent presence felt and to convert their growth plans into reality.

HRM in India is not a new management concept, since it has developed over centuries. The foundations of HRM in India can be traced to the Arlhasastra, a fourth-century BC document referring, among other things, to people management (Chatterjee, 2006). Moreover, British colonial administrations have also left their fingerprint on employment law and HR practices (Chatterjee, 2006). Currently, the influence of globalised markets, which bring international competitive pressures, push Indian companies towards international HR standards. This phenomenon seems to influence Indian SMEs that seek the benefits of internationalisation. Many organisations understand that investing in HRM may be the cornerstone of continued competitiveness (Saini and Budhwar, 2008).

Beyond the aforementioned indications, Indian SMEs are far from being characterised as HRM-centred companies, as they implement less developed HR practices. According to a survey conducted by the Confederation of Indian Industries (Das et al., 2014), 20% of medium and 80% of small-sized businesses have no HR departments. Similarly, in a study of small Indian manufacturing firms, Saini and Budhwar (2008) found that HRM is still informal and achieved through ongoing interpersonal relationships among owners, managers and workers. HRM activities are often neglected by many Indian SMEs. Having said that, India offers more opportunities to introduce HR practices for enhancing staff productivity. Compared to other developed countries where there is the burden of an ageing population, India has a unique window of opportunity called the 'demographic dividend' (Shivesh, 2015). This means that, compared to other large developing and developed countries, India has a higher proportion of working-age individuals in relation to its entire population. India has the opportunity to become a global reservoir of skilled labour, accounting for 28% of the graduate talent pool among 28 of the world's lowest-cost economies (Shivesh, 2015). Among all the countries, India enjoys a unique advantage not only to fulfil its internal demand of skilled labour but also to cater to the labour shortage in other countries. The government is taking proactive steps to fill the existing skill gap in order to influence its position as a supplier of trained human resources to the world.

Indian SME businesses have to develop staff that are capable of taking up challenges thrown by the new economic environment. To tackle this challenging situation, Indian academics and practitioners have advocated the adoption of Human Resource Development (HRD) (Jain et al., 2012). The adoption of professionalised HRD practices in India is a recent phenomenon, but has gained momentum in the past ten years. The contemporary approach of training and development is that Indian SMEs have realised the importance of corporate training (Malik and Nilakant, 2011). Training is considered more of a retention tool rather than a cost.

The significance of HRM in Indian SMEs is demonstrated in the way they have designed HR departments consisting of a vice president of HR, an assistant manager, senior and junior officers and executives, with major strategic enablers identified in terms of recruitment, training, performance appraisal, compensation management, retention strategies and attrition strategies, to name a few (Budhwar et al., 2006). SMEs in India place emphasis on having a well-designed HR department with specific managers and functional specialists. Recruitment activities are gradually becoming dynamic with the practice of external recruitment through recruitment agencies. However, compensation administration is a growing challenge in most SMEs, where compensation strategies are based on factors such as seniority and work experience, individual employee commitment and performance, individual employee skills and competencies or on an amalgamation of all these (Pio, 2007).

In summary, Indian SMEs are progressively witnessing an accelerated growth in the spirit of training and development, and investments in these activities are on the rise. Significant emphasis is placed on the employee relationship component at work and towards developing a smoother communication channel. In addition, talent acquisition strategies are on the rise. At the same time, change management initiatives and interventions are gradually being looked into (Budhwar and Boyne, 2004).

Taiwan

Taiwan is categorised as an advanced emerging economy. Taiwan has developed from a predominantly agriculture-centred country to an industrialised one in less than 40 years (Lin, 1998). Taiwan's SMEs are recognised as the key driving force of the country's economic development for more than half a century (Tai and Huang, 2006). SMEs have played, and continue to play, a crucial role in this economic evolution, especially through innovation, export freedom, creating employment opportunities and laying the foundations of a successful future for SMEs and larger enterprises (Harvie and Lee, 2002). SMEs have supported and developed the economy by integrating the national economy with the global one. In contrast to China and South Korea, Taiwan has typically been viewed as a diverse 'small and medium firm' economy (Bjerke, 2000). Since family-based or family-like relationships dominate and support social interaction in Taiwan, the majority of Taiwanese SMEs are family businesses (Yu, 2009).

The emergence of SMEs in Taiwan is closely associated with domestic conditions, global economic developments, and the government's economic, social and educational policies. For example, to acknowledge the positive economic impact of SMEs, Taiwanese authorities established an SME health centre in 1968 (Xiling, 2009) aiming to promote the development of SMEs by offering guidance to solve financial, technological, production and management dilemmas. Later in 1999, the government introduced the strengthening economic constitution scheme for SMEs (Xiling, 2009) to expand the scope in which SMEs could thrive. For instance, Taiwanese SMEs were viewed by the Nationalist government as a means to overcome the shortages of food and other essential domestic commodities. The expansion of export-oriented SMEs in labour-intensive industries in the 1950s was the result of an effort by the Taiwanese government to use limited state resources to speed up economic growth.

In terms of HRM development in Taiwan, earlier work by Yao (1999) indicates that it has taken place in three stages: Stage I (before the mid-1960s), Stage II (mid 1960s to late 1970s) and Stage III (after the 1980s). In the first stage, HRM was only a part of the administrative function. Its major responsibilities were attendance and leave administration, payroll and employee welfare, hiring and performance appraisal administration. In the second stage, US multinationals (e.g. IBM, RCA, TI) and Japanese multinationals (e.g. Matsushita, Mitsubishi) established operations in Taiwan and transferred their home country's personnel management practices there. During the 1970s, informal professional personnel managers' organisations were formed to meet regularly to exchange personnel information. Here, the function of HRM was operational and reactive. The major responsibilities were hiring and retention, ensuring competitiveness of the job package, providing basic training programmes and maintaining harmonious industrial relations. In the third stage, HRM in Taiwan gradually moved towards involving HR departments in the formulation of business strategies. In this period, two HR professional organisations were formed: the Chinese Human Resource Management Association and the Human Resource Development Association of ROC. Both of them organised and sponsored a number of seminars, workshops and training programmes to promote modern HRM practices. The HRM department has been found to play a strong functional role. Its major responsibilities include personnel planning and control, management training, career development, and providing advice and counsel for line managers (Yao, 1999).

Although SMEs have expanded in Taiwan over the recent years, the HRM function within SMEs is still under development. Many SMEs are family-owned enterprises and rely heavily on Confucianism and informal systems; therefore, they do not have classic HRM functions. It seems that there is a negative connection between family ownership and the adoption of HRM practices (Tsai, 2010) because family-owned firms are less likely to use professional HRM practices (De Kok et al., 2006). Proprietors often serve as managing directors themselves and perform key roles within the firm. Other members of the senior management team are often friends or family of the owner (Marlow, 2005). When HRM practices are adopted, this is often the result of mimetic isomorphic pressures of large or foreign-owned companies (Dacin, 1997). This isomorphic pressures may be rooted in the strong beliefs in Confucianism (a system of social and ethical teachings based on respect and kindness), which enhances social order without the presence of formal rules and regulations (Chen et al., 2008). In this respect, Taiwanese SMEs rarely consider the formalisation of working practices. The main reason for this is that informal interactions offer a range of advantages in a business context, such as speed of decision-making and clear communication channels. Thus, trade union (TU) existence is not necessary. Historically, TUs within Taiwan are weak, yielding and willing to compromise (Boestel, 2002). As conflict is dealt with open communication, most SMEs do not see any benefit of TUs.

Further indicators that Taiwanese SMEs are not keen to adopt formal HRM practices can be observed in the way through training and development is managed. SMEs generally offer limited training and development opportunities due to high turnover rates (Hsiang and Cheng, 2012). The Taiwanese government approached this issue with the intervention of the Occupational Training Fund (1972). This law was passed to coerce any enterprise with more than 40 employees to deduct no less than 1.5% from every employee's remuneration in order to collate a training fund. Due to severe business consequences, this law was replaced in 1983. The revised structure offered a business tax reduction for the uptake of training to encourage the development of such HRM practices. Negandhi (1973) mentions that the HRM practices implemented in local private Taiwanese firms were fewer compared to developed countries. He further indicates that in Taiwanese private firms, HR policies are not stated or documented, independent personnel departments do not exist, job evaluation rarely occurs, selection and promotion criteria are unclear, promotions are based on age and experience, training programmes focus on operatives only and financial rewards are the main incentives used.

Later research by Yeh (1991) found that the HRM practices of Taiwanese firms are a kind of mixture of practices imported from Japan and America. He argues that local firms in Taiwan have adapted very well in people management and can no longer be considered as less developed. He also suggests that adaptation and learning from the US and Japan have increased managerial ability in local private Taiwanese firms in utilising their HR. Due to the small size of SMEs, importance is placed on perceptions of individual managers to control overall decision-making while aiming to diminish the role of formal rules and systems (Lu and Beamish, 2001). An example of this is recruitment and selection. While this function is practiced within SMEs, the process is often unorthodox. In Taiwanese SMEs, when shortlisting candidates, value is placed on loyalty and personality rather than skill or qualification. Many candidates are recruited through word of mouth or referrals (Chen et al., 2008). Due to Confucianism, there is a striking resemblance to HRM in SMEs and that of larger organisations, with the exception of grievance procedures, job security and certain recruitment methods. While rewards and compensation are commonplace, SMEs in Taiwan only offer such incentives to certain occupational groups (Tsai, 2010).

Furthermore, Taiwan has been famous for harmonious industrial relations in achieving successful economic development. TUs in Taiwan are categorised into two types: industrial unions and craft unions. Even though craft unions have a higher organisation rate, their role in industrial relations is less important. This is because the major reason for a worker to join a craft union is to join the labour insurance programme which is subsidised by the government (Chen, 1998). The low organisation rate of industrial unions can be attributed to the high proportion of SMEs and the high turnover rates in business (Chen, 1998). In Taiwanese SMEs, even though there is an agreement between the union and employer, many union members get only a tiny benefit, such as one more paid holiday from the employers. It is suggested that unions in Taiwan are concerned more with the provision of services and social activities for members and rarely involve themselves in collective bargaining or in promoting improvements in working conditions (Lin, 1997).

Despite the overall negative evidence regarding the application of HRM in Taiwanese SMEs, there are some more recent evidence suggesting the opposite. For example, Tsai (2010) argues that the state of HRM in Taiwanese SMEs is in much better shape than is assumed. In particular, he claims that Taiwanese SMEs pay great attention to talent management, through solid trainings for employee development, reward packages, suggestions for improvement, recognition and appraisals. However, he points out that despite the developments in the HRM field, progress is slow.

In summary, there are both cultural and institutional factors influencing the development of HRM practices in SMEs in Taiwan. HRM in Taiwanese SMEs seems to be limited due to a desire for deregulation influenced by culture, values and beliefs that characterise this emerging economy. Nevertheless, as in other cases, it seems that lately there are some positive indicators towards the adoption of various HRM practices, although progress is slow.

Vietnam

Vietnam's economic system is currently in transition. Since December 1986, the country has gradually transferred from a command economy to a market economy. Although it experienced some difficulties during the transition period, Vietnam has achieved remarkable results. GDP growth rate in Vietnam averaged 6.2% from 2000 until 2018, reaching an all-time high of 8.46% in 2007 (Trading Economics, 2018). This transformation occurred in both the public and private sectors. The

Vietnamese State recognises private enterprises as an integral part of a 'multi-sector' economy and has passed laws promoting the development of such enterprises. This has led to an increase in the number of formal private enterprises (Webster, 1999), which have been identified as the main engine of the economy (World Bank, 1999; Zhu et al., 2007).

SMEs operating in Vietnam face several unique circumstances that impact upon the adoption of HRM practices. Vietnam has a predominately collective culture which emphasises social relationships (Nguyen and Bryant, 2004). SMEs in Vietnam are also predominately family businesses comprised of immediate and extended family members within the business itself and within their suppliers and customers (Bagwell, 2008). This family network dominates much of the business practices of these SMEs. These close personal ties with family members reduce the likelihood that firms will adopt formal HR practices to manage employee relationships. Rather, appeals to family loyalty and the good of the family business will take precedence over individual needs. Furthermore, Vietnam has underdeveloped market institutions (courts, regulation bodies, certification agencies) to oversee business transactions (Richardson, 2008). Consequently, SMEs rely on personal knowledge and family ties to make transactions safer and more reliable. This lack of government regulation concerning employment further justifies the informal practices.

There are several factors driving formalised employment relations in Vietnamese SMEs (Webster, 1999): first, competition from international firms and state-owned enterprises; second, expectations from international business partners or customers; and third, pressure from banks to formalise HR practices in order to qualify for loans, etc. SMEs in Vietnam compete with and operate alongside larger state-owned enterprises and large international firms. Webster (1999) explains that the most common perceptions of private firms and their owners are that they are unstable and vulnerable to bankruptcy, exploitive of their labour, dishonest and opportunistic. In his study, SMEs were the least attractive employers when compared to the government, state-owned enterprises and foreign companies. They were seen as poor job options because they were deemed unstable, unable to offer job security and without career development and training opportunities (Webster, 1999). Similarly, Vietnamese workers would rather prefer to work for these larger, more established firms. These firms tend to provide better pay, formal systems for hiring, firing and evaluating performance, and opportunities for advancement. Consequently, Vietnamese SMEs feel pressure to provide some of these same services for their employees to compete for good employees.

SMEs in Vietnam with informal HR practices are not perceived as good loan applicants by senior credit officers (Ram et al., 2001). Bank officials in Vietnam perceive SMEs with low HR formality to be unreliable and lacking transparency in management, which can be translated into high risk for misusing the loans (Nguyen et al., 2004). In order to qualify for loans from these institutions, private SMEs feel pressure to formalise some of their HR practices. Thus, decisions on the level of HR practices are influenced by a complex set of cultural, economic and institutional factors (Ram et al., 2001).

Moreover, it seems that there is an enhanced HR function when SMEs collaborate directly with foreign firms. The latter usually have strong influences on HR functions of the former (Rainnie, 1989). Most manufacturing firms produce low-entry barrier, low-margin products within export industries, such as garment and footwear (Webster, 1999). In most cases, orders from foreign firms are large in quantity but low in margin (Luong, 2001). This creates a need for SMEs to have strong controls over their labour processes because these firms are actually selling Vietnamese labour. In the late 1990s, foreign firms have become cautious about their Vietnamese subcontractors' HR practices. They require their Vietnamese subcontractors to have some formal HR policies (e.g. minimum wages, clear grievance systems, good working conditions). This has pushed Vietnamese SMEs to formalise their HR practices. For example, Castrol Vietnam Ltd., a distributing company in Vietnam, trimmed down its number of distributors, who were all private SMEs, from 180 to 80 (Nguyen and Bryant, 2004). Its management was concerned that the lack of professionalism in their distributor's management had negatively influenced Castrol's brand image. For the remaining 80 distributors, the company actively helped them improve their management practices, from business planning and selling practices to HR policies (Nguyen and Bryant, 2004). Thus, foreign firms have created both pressures and incentives for their SME partners to adopt formal professional management practices.

In summary, in Vietnam, as in other cases of emerging economies, there are both strong cultural and institutional factors influencing HR applications in SMEs. HRM is informal in most of the cases. However, synergies with large companies can possibly create the context within which SMEs can adopt and develop formal HR practices that can help them modernise their operations. Currently, this seems to be more evident in the manufacturing sector.

Indonesia

Indonesia is the fourth most populous country in the world, with about 234.6 million people. The size of the labour force is approximately 108.2 million. It consists of almost 17,508 islands and islets, making it a large archipelago. Reports on HRM in Indonesia are limited (Bennington and Habir, 2003). SMEs have historically been viewed as the main players in the Indonesian economy especially because they are a large provider of employment opportunities and a source of economic growth and foreign currency earnings. Typically, Indonesian SMEs account for more than 90% of all firms and provide livelihood for over 90% of the country's workforce (Tambunan, 2007).

Indonesia's high score on power distance indicates a work culture that is dictated by clear organisational hierarchies (Tarmidi, 1999). There is a predominance of males in upper-level management positions, and gender discrimination in the workplace is common.

Traditionally, family connections have been widely used by local private organisations as a means of recruitment in Indonesia (Tabalujan, 2002). Current states of practices indicate the use of multiple recruitment methods such as word of mouth, print advertisements, newspapers, magazines, commercial broadcasts, recruitment consultants and the Internet. The most common recruitment method used for blue-collar workers is word of mouth. According to Huo et al. (2002), a person's ability to perform the technical requirements of the job, an interview and an employment test are the main selection practices. Earlier research by Galang (1999) had revealed that SMEs and large enterprises in Indonesia do not differ significantly except in retention practices, where large companies focus on hiring employees on a long-term basis. However, according to findings by Galang (1999) and Huo et al. (2002), the ability to perform technical job requirements and the ability to get along well with others are both important hiring criteria. As far as preferred recruitment practices are concerned, Huo et al. (2002) found that a person's ability to perform the technical requirements of the job, a person's ability to get along well with others, and a person's potential to do a good job are among the top-ranked preferred selection criteria in Indonesia.

The Indonesian government promotes various forms of vocational and on-the-job training programmes, including nine years of compulsory education for every Indonesian citizen (Prijadi and Rachmawathi, 2002). Skill training is available through vocational senior secondary schools (which account for more than 1.3 million of senior secondary enrolments), 153 public training centres, (which offer short, specialised courses) and numerous privately run programmes. Mohamad et al. (2012) reveal that SMEs in Indonesia provide in-house training for employees and encourage them to attend external skill training programmes usually provided by government agencies. In addition, in a ten-country comparative study of SMEs and large-scale companies, Drost et al. (2002) found that Indonesia scored the lowest in current training investment for technical skills improvement and that Indonesia uses training as a mean of rewarding employees. Furthermore, Indonesia ranked very low in the utilisation of training for improving interpersonal skills. However, Indonesia ranked high in providing training for improving poor employee performance (Robinson et al., 2001).

In terms of performance appraisal systems, these vary across organisations from a management-by-objectives (MBO) approach to upward and 360-degree feedback (Bennington and Habir, 2003). Earlier work by Galang (1999) found that appraisals in Indonesia usually recognise good performance, identify development activities and allow subordinates to express their perspectives and feelings. However, research by Milliman et al. (2002) on the purpose of performance appraisals in the US and the Pacific Rim found that firms in Indonesia place low emphasis on performance appraisals. The main concerns of most Indonesian organisations relate to productivity and quality. For example, Bennington and Habir (2003) report that output per worker in Indonesia is about one-quarter of that of other developing countries like Korea and one-tenth of that of the US.

As far as reward strategies is concerned, these are perceived as costly and for this reason their application is rare (Wright et al., 2005b). In addition, there is little transparency in compensation systems used in both public and private sectors in Indonesia (Bennington and Habir, 2003). For white-collar workers and managers, pay and benefits are an important consideration in deciding whether to work for a particular enterprise. Since labour supply always exceeds demand, blue-collar workers do not have as many options to choose from and face difficulties in exercising bargaining power over wages. Despite that, the government in Indonesia has established regional minimum wages. However, blue-collar workers are often unable to turn down work at rates below the minimum (Prijadi and Rachmawathi, 2002).

Finally, there are great differences between the lowest and highest paid employees in SMEs in Indonesia. Lowe et al. (2002) report that the use of job performance as the basis of pay raises and pay incentives (bonus or profit sharing) is relatively low in Indonesia. Despite the fact that Indonesia is one of the highest ranked collectivistic countries in Asia, the degree to which pay is contingent on group performance is also relatively low. An employee's seniority forms an important part of the total pay package in Indonesian SMEs. However, there is a relatively low level of recognition of long-term results and futuristic orientation of their pay policies.

In summary, HRM in Indonesia is mainly informal and underdeveloped in SMEs. There is evidence, though, of application of HRM practices, such as recruitment, training and development, performance management and rewards, albeit that these are not always effectively applied. One more time, the influence of institutions as well as large MNCs can be substantial in influencing the implementation of more formalised HR practices by Indonesian SMEs.

South Korea

South Korea has demonstrated incredible growth and global integration to become a high-tech industrialised economy. The country has adopted various economic reforms following the 2008 financial crisis, including greater openness to foreign investment and imports. South Korea is the world's largest manufacturer of DRAMS (Direct Random Access Memory chips), the world's second largest manufacturer in shipbuilding, and the fourth largest electronic industry (Gross, and Connor, 2008). South Korean SMEs can be classified as either ordinary or venture. The differences in these two types are in their management and strategic priorities. A venture SME is defined as an enterprise or organisation that is technology-intensive, or an enterprise based on a highly advanced technology (Gregory et al., 2002).

The government has paid increased attention to the development of SMEs since 1990s. SMEs in South Korea have been playing a vital role in job creation, income generation, technological innovations and improved product quality. SMEs in the manufacturing sector comprise 99.7% of all enterprises and provide 74.3% of the total manufacturing employment. They are considered the backbone of the economy (Gregory et al., 2002). In 2009, the Korean Federation of Small Business indicated that the total number of SMEs accounted for 99.9% of the total number of businesses.

The South Korean work culture has a high score in power distance, emphasising clear differentiation between superiors and subordinates (Dastmalchian et al., 2000). The culture is low on individualism, and this implies a collective spirit and the importance of harmony at the workplace. The culture is considered feminine as men's and women's roles generally overlap and the society tends to be nurturing and modest (An and Kim, 2007).

In South Korea, SMEs rely less on external recruitment and testing and more on personnel connections in recruiting blue-collar employees, particularly in SMEs located in rural areas. One common method of recruitment in South Korea is based on relationships and networking. Family members, relatives, friends and alumni are often good sources for referrals and recruitment (Gross and Connor, 2008). Kotey and Folker (2007) point out that training of employees in SMEs in South Korea is usually informal, not planned, with minimum dispositions and with a short-term orientation. Formally offering employee training is perceived as an added cost (Mayson and Barrett, 2006). In South Korea, there has been evidence of considerable efforts made by organisations to develop employees at all levels (Bae et al., 2003). This is partly due to the fact that South Korean organisations consider HR to be the central building block for long-term corporate success. The orientation towards work, helping employees understand the business and teaching employees about company values are all important training objectives in South Korean SMEs.

The most commonly used performance appraisal methods in South Korean SMEs are graphic rating scales and the essay evaluation method (Milliman et al., 2002). Lowe et al. (2002) proclaim that employees expect a relatively high level of pay incentives, a futuristic orientation,

seniority, long-term results and reward packages that rely on job performance. According to Lowe at al. (2002), incentives, seniority and job
performance are among the top three components of the reward system
used by SMEs in South Korea.

In summary, South Korean SMEs use a mix of formal and informal HR
practices targeted at increasing their efficiency and effectiveness in respond-
ing to changing government regulations and market competition pressures.

Summary

Chapter 3 focused on EMEs in Asia and the Pacific, particularly on the
role of SMEs and HRM in this context. HRM in SMEs in emerging
markets is undergoing transition. This transition is influenced by historical, cultural and institutional factors, which determine the way in
which HRM is implemented. In addition, it seems that in some cases,
either organisational size (mainly medium) or the sector that SMEs
operate in (like manufacturing) play a significant role in the formal
adoption of HRM logics and practices. In China, there is evidence of
modernisation and formalisation of HRM and employment practices
in SMEs due to the internationalisation of businesses in recent years.
Of course, the influence of both culture and institutions over the application of Western-type HR practices is enormous. Similarly, SMEs in
India are progressively experiencing an accelerated growth in the use
of HRM practices, such as training and development and talent management. However, the progress of HR in SMEs in India is affected by
both cultural and strong institutional aspects that cannot be neglected.
In Taiwan, HRM application is limited due to cultural factors and to
the high proportion of family-owned enterprises that rely on informal
systems of management. However, there is some limited evidence of a
slower progress towards the implementation of HRM in local SMEs. In
Vietnam, HRM formalisation in SMEs depends upon several factors,
such as competition from international firms and state-owned enterprises, expectations from international business partners or customers,
and pressure from banks. Finally, in South Korea, there is evidence of
HRM formalisation; however, this is not consistent across enterprises.
The next chapter focuses on EMEs in Africa.

References

An, D. and Kim, S. (2007). Relating Hofstede's masculinity dimension to
gender role portrayals in advertising: A cross-cultural comparison of web
advertisements. *International Marketing Review*, 24(2): pp. 181–207.
Au, A. K. M., Altman, Y. and Roussel, J. (2008). Employee training needs
and perceived value of training in the Pearl River Delta of China: A human
capital development approach. *Journal of European Industrial Training*, 32(1):
pp. 19–31.

Aycan, Z. (2004). Leadership and teamwork in the developing country context. In H. W. Lane, M. L. Maznevski, M. E. Mendenhall and J. McNett, eds., *Handbook of Global Management: A Guide to Managing Complexity*. Oxford: Blackwell Publishing Ltd., pp. 406–422.

Bae, J., Chen, S., Wan, D., Lawler, J. and Walumbwa, F. (2003). Human resource strategy and firm performance in Pacific Rim countries. *International Journal of Human Resource Management*, 14: pp. 1308–1332.

Bagwell, S. (2008). Transnational family networks and ethnic minority business development: The case of Vietnamese nail-shops in the UK. *International Journal of Entrepreneurial Behaviour and Research*, 14(6): pp. 377–394.

Bennington, L. and Habir, A. D. (2003). Human resource management in Indonesia. *Human Resource Management Review*, 13: pp. 373–392.

Bjerke, B. (2000). A typified, culture-based, interpretation of management of SMEs in Southeast Asia. *Asia Pacific Journal of Management*, 17: pp. 103–132.

Bjorkman, I. and Fan, X. (2002). Human resource management and the performance of Western firms in China. *International Journal of Human Resource Management*, 13(6): pp. 853–864.

Boestel, J. (2002). Management in Taiwan. In M. Warner, ed., *International Encyclopedia of Business and Management*. (2nd edition). London: Thomson Learning, pp. 6325–6330.

Bond, M. H. (1996). Chinese values. In M. H. Bond, ed., *The Handbook of Chinese Psychology*. New York: Oxford University Press, pp. 208–226.

Bruton, G. D., Ahlstrom, D. and Obloj, K. (2008). Entrepreneurship in emerging economies: Where are we today and where should the research go in the future. *Entrepreneurship Theory and Practice*, 32(1): pp. 1–14.

Budhwar, P. S. and Boyne, G. (2004). Human resource management in the Indian public and private sectors: An empirical comparison. *The International Journal of Human Resource Management*, 15(2): pp. 346–370.

Budhwar, P. S., Varma, A., Singh, V. and Dhar, R. (2006). HRM systems of Indian call centres: An exploratory study. *The International Journal of Human Resource Management*, 17(5): pp. 881–897.

Cappelli, P. (2008). *Talent on Demand: Managing Talent in an Age of Uncertainty*. Boston, MA: Harvard Business Press.

Chatterjee, S. R. (2006). Human resource management in India. In A. Nankervis, S. R. Chatterjee and J. Coffey, eds., *Perspectives of Human Resource Management in the Asia Pacific*. Malaysia: Pearson Prentice Hall, pp. 41–62.

Chen, R., Sun, C., Helms, M. and Jih, W. (2008). Role negotiation and interaction: An exploratory case study of the impact of management consultants on ERP system implementation in SMEs in Taiwan. *Information Systems Management*, 25(2): pp. 159–173.

Chen, S.J. (1998). The development of HRM practices in Taiwan. In C. Rowley, ed., *Human Resource Management in the Asia Pacific Region: Convergence Questioned*. London: Frank Cass, pp. 152–169.

Child, J. (1991). A foreign perspective on the management of people in China. *International Journal of Human Resource Management*, 2: pp. 93–107.

Cooke, F. L. (2005). *HRM, Work and Employment in China*. London and New York: Routledge.

Cooke, F. L., Wood, G., Psychogios, A. and Szamosi, T. L. (2011). HRM in emergent market economies: Evidence and implications from Europe. *Human Resource Management Journal*, 21(4): pp. 368–378.

Cox, S. (2017). *Defining Emerging Markets*. The Economist [online]. Available at: https://www.economist.com/special-report/2017/10/07/defining-emerging-markets. [Accessed 1 November 2018].

Cui, W., Khan, Z. and Tarba, S. Y. (2018). Strategic Talent Management in Service SMEs of China. *Thunderbird International Business Review*, 60(1): pp. 9–20.

Dacin, M. T. (1997). Isomorphism in context: The power and prescription of institutional norms. *Academy of Management Journal*, 40(1): pp. 46–81.

Das, S. P., Narendra, P. and Mishra, P. (2014). HR issues in small and medium enterprises: A literature review. *IMPACT: International Journal of Research in Humanities, Arts and Literature*, 2(5): pp. 183–194.

Dastmalchian, A., Lee, S. and Ng, I. (2000). The interplay between organisational and national cultures: A comparison of organisational practices in Canada and South Korea using the competing values framework. *International Journal of Human Resource Management*, 11(2): pp. 388–412.

De Kok, J. M. P., Uhlaner, L. M. and Thurik, A. R. (2006). Professional HRM practices in family owned-managed enterprises. *Journal of Small Business Management*, 44(3): pp. 441–460.

Drost, A. E., Frayne, C. A., Lowe, K. B. and Geringer, M. J. (2002). Benchmarking training and development practices: A multi-country comparative analysis. *Human Resource Management*, 41(1): pp. 67–86.

Easterby-Smith, M., Malina, D. and Yuan, L. (1995). How culture sensitive is HRM? A comparative analysis of practice in Chinese and UK companies. *International Journal of Human Resource Management*, 6(1): pp. 31–59.

Emerging Economy Report (2008). Available at: http://cks.in/portfolio-item/emerging-economy-report/.

Financial Dictionary (2018). Available at: www.investinganswers.com/financial-dictionary/world-markets/emerging-market-economy-1518.

Galang, M. C. (1999). HRM practices in small enterprises in selected Asian countries: How do they compare with larger enterprises? *Human Resource Management Symposium on SMEs*, A6: pp. 1–17.

Gao, Q. and Banerji, S. (2015). The growth appraisal system for Chinese SMEs. *Journal of Chinese Economic and Business Studies*, 13(2): pp. 175–193.

Gregory, G., Harvie, C. and Lee, H. H. (2002). Korean SMEs in the twenty first century: Strategies, constraints, and performance in a global economy. *Economic Papers*, 21(3): pp. 64–79.

Gross, A. and Connor, A. (2008). *HR, Recruiting Trends in South Korea* [online]. Available at: https://www.shrm.org/resourcesandtools/hr-topics/global-hr/pages/hr,recruitinginsouthkorea.aspx. [Accessed 1 November 2018].

Hamel, G. (2009). Moon shots for management. *Harvard Business Review*, 87(2): pp. 91–102.

Harvie, C. and Lee, B. (2002). *The Role of SMEs in National Economies in East Asia*. (Vol. 2). Cheltenham: Edward Elgar Publishing.

Heakal, R. (2017). *What is an emerging market economy?* [online]. Available at: www.investopedia.com/articles/03/073003.asp. [Accessed 1 September 2018].

Hoffmann, R. (2017). *SMEs in China*. [online]. Available at: www.ecovis-beijing. com/en/blog-en/articles/887-smes-in-china. [Accessed 1 September 2018].

Hofstede, G. (1980). *Culture's Consequences: International Differences in Work-Related Values*. Newbury Park, CA: Sage.

Hsiang, L. and Cheng, C. (2012). Adoption of practices by subsidiaries and institutional interaction within internationalised small- and medium-sized enterprises. *Management International Review*, 52: pp. 81–105.

Huo, Y. P., Huang, H. and Napier, N. (2002). Divergence or convergence: A cross-national comparison of personnel selection practices. *Human Resource Management*, 41(1): p. 3144.

Huo, Y. P. and Von Glinow, M. A. V. (1995). On transplanting human resource practices to China: A culture-driven approach. *International Journal of Manpower*, 16(9): pp. 3–15.

Jain, H., Budhwar, P., Varma, A. and Ratnam, C. V. (2012). Human resource management in the new economy in India. *The International Journal of Human Resource Management*, 23(5): pp. 887–891.

Khavul, S., Benson, G. S. and Datta, D. K. (2010). Is internationalisation associated with investments in HRM? A study of entrepreneurial firms in emerging markets. *Human Resource Management*, 49(4): pp. 693–713.

Ko, W. W. and Liu, G. (2017). Overcoming the liability of smallness by recruiting through networks in China: A guanxi-based social capital perspective. *The International Journal of Human Resource Management*, 28(11): pp. 1499–1526.

Kotey, B. and Folker, C. (2007). Employee training in SMEs: Effect of size and firm type – family and nonfamily. *Journal of Small Business Management*, 45(2): pp. 214–238.

Kvint, V. (2009). *The Global Emerging Market: Strategic Management and Economics*. London and New York: Routledge.

Lin, C. (1998). Success factors of small-and medium-sized enterprises in Taiwan: An analysis of cases. *Journal of Small Business Management*, 36(4): p. 43.

Lin, Y. Y. (1997). Labour relations in Taiwan: A cross-cultural perspective. *Industrial Relations Journal*, 28(1): pp. 56–67.

Liu, X., Potocnik, K. and Anderson, N. (2016). Applicant reactions to selection methods in China. *International Journal of Selection and Assessment*, 24(3): pp. 296–303.

Lowe, K. B., Milliman, J., DeCieri, H. and Dowling, P. J. (2002). International compensation practices: A ten-country comparative analysis. *Human Resource Management*, 41(1): pp. 45–66.

Lu, J. W. and Beamish, P. W. (2001). The internationalisation and performance of SMEs. *Strategic Management Journal*, 22(6/7): pp. 565–586.

Luong, H. V. (2001). The strength of Vietnamese industrial fabric: Institutional mechanisms of firm competitiveness in the textile and garment industries in Vietnam. *Journal of Asian Business*, 17(1): pp. 17–44.

Malik, A. and Nilakant, V. (2011). Extending the 'size matters' debate: Drivers of training in three business process outsourcing SMEs in India. *Management Research Review*, 34(1): pp. 111–132.

Marlow, S. (2005). Introduction. In S. Marlow, D. Patton and M. Ram, eds., *Labour Management in Small Firms*. London: Routledge.

Marois, T. (2012). *States, Banks and Crisis: Emerging Finance Capitalism in Mexico and Turkey*. Cheltenham: Edward Elgar.

Mayson, S. and Barrett, R. (2006). The science and practice of HRM in small firms. *Human Resources Management Review*, 16: pp. 447–455.

Mazzarol, T. (2003). A model of small business HR growth management. *International Journal of Entrepreneurial Behaviour and Research*, 9(1): pp. 27–49.

Milliman, J., Nason, S., Zhu, C. and De Cieri, H. (2002). An exploratory assessment of the purposes of performance appraisals in North and Central America and the Pacific Rim. *Human Resource Management*, 41(1): pp. 87–102.

Negandhi, A. R. (1973). *Management and Economic Development: The Case of Taiwan*. The Hague, Netherlands: Martinus Nijhoff.

Nguyen, T. V. and Bryant, S. E. (2004). A study of the formality of human resource management practices in small and medium-size enterprises in Vietnam. *International Small Business Journal*, 22(6): pp. 595–618.

Nguyen, T. V., Le, T. B. N. and Freeman, N. (2004). *Coping with Uncertainty: Understanding How Banks Lend to Private Small- and Medium-Sized Enterprises (SMEs) in Vietnam*. Hanoi: Asian Institute of Management, National Economics University.

Pio, E. (2007). HRM and Indian epistemologies: A review and avenues for future research. *Human Resource Management Review*, 17(3): pp. 319–335.

Prijadi, R. and Rachmawati, R. (2002). Indonesia. In M. Zanko, ed., *The Handbook of Human Resource Management Policies and Practices in Asia-Pacific Economies*. Cheltenham, Edward Edgar Publishing Ltd., pp. 260–293.

Psychogios, A. G., Prouska, R. and Brewster, C. (2016). A Three-fold framework for understanding HRM practices in South-Eastern European SMEs. *Employee Relations*, 38(3): pp. 310–331.

Punnett, B. J. (2004). The developing world: Toward a managerial understanding. In H. W. Lane, M. L. Maznevski, M. E. Mendenhall and J. McNett, eds., *Handbook of Global Management: A Guide to Managing Complexity*. Oxford: Blackwell Publishing Ltd., pp. 406–422.

Rainnie, A. (1989). *Industrial Relations in Small Firms: Small Isn't Beautiful*. London: Routledge.

Ram, M., Marlow, A. and Patton, D. (2001). Managing the locals: Employee relations in South Asian restaurants. *Entrepreneurship and Regional Development*, 13(3): pp. 229–245.

Richardson, B. J. (2008). *Socially Responsible Investment Law: Regulating the Unseen Polluters*. Oxford: Oxford University Press.

Robinson, J. S., Burkhalter, B. R., Rasmussen, B. and Sugiono, R. (2001). Low-cost on-the-job peer training of nurses improved immunisation coverage in Indonesia. *Bulletin of the World Health Organisation*, 79: pp. 150–158.

Mohamad, M. R., Kuswantoro, F. and Omar, A. R. C. (2012). *Competitive strategies and firm performance: A comparative study of Malaysian and Indonesian SMEs*. In 3rd International Conference on Business and Economic Research (3rd ICBER 2012) Proceedings. Selangor, Malaysia: Global Research Agency, pp. 460–474.

Rowley, C. and Benson, J. (2003). Introduction: Changes and continuities in Asian HRM. *Asia Pacific Business Review*, 9(4): pp. 1–14.

Saini, D. S. and Budhwar, P. S. (2008). Managing the human resource in Indian SMEs: The role of indigenous realities. *Journal of World Business*, 43(4): pp. 417–434.

Shivesh, P. (2015). Demographic dividend: The rich source of skilled people in India. *International Journal of Management and Development*, 2(12): pp. 31–36.

Tabalujan, B. S. (2002). Family capitalism and corporate governance of family-controlled listed companies in Indonesia. *UNSWLJ*, 25: p. 486.

Tai, D. and Huang, C. (2006). A study on relations between industrial transformation and performance of Taiwan's small and medium enterprises. *The Journal of American Academy of Business*, 8(2): pp. 216–221.

Tambunan, T. T. H. (2007). *Entrepreneurship Development in Developing Countries*. New Delhi: Academic Excellence.

Tang, J. and Ward, A. (2003). *The Changing Face of Chinese Management*. London: Routledge.

Tarmidi, L. T. (1999). *Strategies for HRM of SMEs in Indonesia*. Asia-Pacific Economic Cooperation, Human Resource Management Symposium on SMEs, Vol. 2. [online]. Available at: http://citeseerx.ist.psu.edu/viewdoc/download?doi=10.1.1.473.8677&rep=rep1&type=pdf#page=5. [Accessed 1 September 2018].

Trading Economics (2018). *Vietnam GDP growth rate 2000–2018*. [online]. Available at: https://tradingeconomics.com/vietnam/gdp-growth. [Accessed 1 September 2018].

Tsai, C. J. (2010). HRM in SMEs: Homogeneity or heterogeneity? A study of Taiwanese high-tech firms. *The International Journal of Human Resource Management*, 21(10): pp. 1689–1711.

Tung, R. L. and Aycan, Z. (2008). Key success factors and indigenous management practices in SMEs in emerging economies. *Journal of World Business*, 43: pp. 381–384.

Tyagarajan, N. (2013). The great global talent hunt. *Financial Executive*, 29(6): pp. 48–50.

Verburg, R. (1996). Developing HRM in Foreign-Chinese joint ventures. *European Management Journal*, 14(5): pp. 518–525.

Webster, L. (1999). *SIMEs in Vietnam: On the Road to Prosperity. MPDF Private Sector Discussion No. 10*. Hanoi: Mekong Private Sector Development Facility.

Whitley, R. (1992). *Business Systems in East Asia: Firms, Markets, and Societies*. London: Sage.

Wilhelm, P. G. and Xia, A. (1993). A comparison of the United States and Chinese managerial cultures in a transnational period: Implications for labour relations and joint ventures. *International Journal of Organisational Analysis*, 1(4): pp. 405–426.

Williams, C. C. (2014). Out of the shadows: A classification of economies by the size and character of their informal sector. *Work, Employment and Society*, 28(5): pp. 735–753.

Williams, C. C. and Nadin, S. (2010). Entrepreneurship and the informal economy: An overview. *Journal of Developmental Entrepreneurship*, 15(4): pp. 361–378.

Wood, G., Psychogios, A. G. and Fotopoulou, D. (2007). *A Londoner in Athens: Transferring Anglo-Saxon management knowledge to Non-Anglo-Saxon business systems*. 23rd EGOS Colloquium: Beyond Waltz – Dances of Individuals and Organisation, Vienna University of Economics and Business Administration, Vienna, Austria.

World Bank (1999). *Vietnam Preparing for Take-off? How Vietnam can Participate Fully in the East Asian Recovery*. Hanoi: World Bank.

Wright, P. M., Filatotchev, I., Hoskisson, R. E. and Peng, M. W. (2005a). Strategy research in emerging economies: Challenging the conventional wisdom. *Journal of Management Studies*, 42(1): pp. 1–33.

Wright, P. M., Snell, S. A. and Dyer, L. (2005b). New models of strategic HRM in a global context. *The International Journal of Human Resource Management*, 16(6): pp. 875–881.

Xiling, L. (2009). *Comparative Study of SME Between Taiwan and China Mainland*. Beijing: Union University, College of Management.

Yan, Y. (2003). A comparative study of human resource management practices in international joint ventures: The impact of national origin. *International Journal of Human Resource Management*, 14(4): pp. 487–510.

Yao, D. (1999). *Human Resource Management Challenges in Chinese Taipei*. Human Resource Management Symposium on SMEs Proceedings. (Vol. 2). Kaoshung: National Sun Yat-sen University.

Yeh, R. S. (1991). Management practices of Taiwanese firms: As compared to those of American and Japanese subsidiaries in Taiwan. *Asia Pacific Journal of Management*, 8(1): pp. 1–14.

Yu, F.-L. T. (2009). Towards a structural model of a small family business in Taiwan. *Journal of Small Business and Entrepreneurship*, 22(4): pp. 413–428.

Zheng, C., O'Neill, G. and Morrison, M. (2009). Enhancing Chinese SME performance through innovative HR practices. *Personnel Review*, 38(2): pp. 175–194.

Zhu, C. J. H. and Dowling, P. J. (2002). Staffing practices in transition: Some empirical evidence in China. *International Journal of Human Resource Management*, 13: pp. 569–597.

Zhu, Y., Warner, M. and Rowley, C. (2007). Human resource management with 'Asian' characteristics: A hybrid people-management system in East Asia. *The International Journal of Human Resource Management*, 18(5): pp. 745–768.

4 HRM in SMEs in Emerging Market Economies II – Africa

Introduction

This chapter explores HRM practices applied by SMEs in a group of emerging economies in Africa. In particular, the chapter focuses on South Africa, Ghana, Nigeria and Algeria. At the time of writing, there was a lack of concrete and reliable research evidence of HRM in SMEs in the majority of African economies. This is the reason why we do not include other African countries in this chapter, but only those for which we have found some critical studies.

Africa has witnessed great economic changes in recent years. By 2035, the number of Africans joining the working-age population will exceed that of the rest of the world combined (Vollgraaff, 2015). SMEs are at the heart of employment expansion, creating around 80% of the region's employment (World Economic Forum, 2015). Given their importance to job creation, product and service innovation and overall economic progress, it is crucial that HRM in SMEs within the African context is studied in order to help these small and medium firms achieve further growth. This chapter continues the discussion on HRM in SMEs in emerging economies.

South Africa

The National Small Business Development (NSBD) Strategy (1995) of South Africa asserts that SMEs are companies with fewer than 100 employees (Ladzani and Van Vuuren, 2002). Most SMEs in South Africa are well established, formally registered, have fixed business premises and are usually managed by the owner with decentralised management structures and division of labour. In this respect, South African SMEs have particular characteristics which are inextricably linked to the specifications as laid down by the NSBD Act 102 of 1996 amended by Act 29 of 2004 (Ladzani and Van Vuuren, 2002). The NSBD Act further categorises small businesses in South Africa into distinct groups, namely micro, very small, small and medium. Despite the effort, though, SMEs in South Africa have achieved limited development and growth (Fatoki and Asah, 2011; Olawale and Garwe, 2010). The reasons can be rooted, among other things, in the strong influence by the apartheid regime.

South Africa's apartheid regime influenced employment practices and HRM in general (Sakar, 2007). During the period of apartheid, the government determined, to a great degree, employment practices mainly based on race. This tradition still influences the post-apartheid South African HRM context. From the moment that multinational corporations started to invest (mainly after 1994), new management methods were transferred and, consequently, influenced the local business agenda. However, it seems that South African SMEs are far from being characterised as HRM-oriented. There is a lack of HR planning complimented by a lack of supportive organisational culture, which inhibits HR development within South African SMEs. Smit and Watkins (2012) argue that entrepreneurs prefer to avoid taking risks, but they fail to take into account that every risk pattern has an effect on their operations. Most of their actions are centred on avoiding risks rather than devising HR planning initiatives. In addition, strategic HR planning is severely undermined by the lack of reliable information. The effects are that HR strategy and policy are often formulated in an *ad hoc* manner and internal practices are not properly evaluated (Bowmaker-Falconer and Day, 1995). Furthermore, a failure to understand and implement policies related to entrepreneurial activities can yield negative results for SMEs in South Africa. As such, when entrepreneurs adopt a proactive business approach, the outcome is business success through novelty, positive transfer of learning, target-setting and achievement (Smit and Watkins, 2012).

Similarly, the process of recruiting and selecting employees varies in SMEs in South Africa. Some of them do not have clear policies and procedures. As such, recruitment and selection is often done along family lines or referrals. One reason for this is that some business owners are sceptical about recruiting outsiders (Long et al., 2014). This, according to Van Scheers (2011), results in a lack of proper structure for recruitment and selection practices. In terms of employment equality, research by Bowmaker-Falconer et al. (1998) discuss that, historically, the labour market was a distorted one, with inequality in access to education, skills, managerial and professional work based on race and ethnicity. However, equal opportunity programmes in South Africa have led to changes in internal labour markets of medium and large organisations.

The lack of specific resourcing practices seems to have an impact on compensation and talent management. SMEs in South Africa often lack the financial resources required to retain talented employees (Long et al., 2014). At the same time, the majority of South Africans do not want to become entrepreneurs, preferring to enter the job market as employees (Rogerson, 2009).

As far as reward strategies are concerned, these are affected by shrinking markets. For example, 28% of SMEs in South Africa reduced their labour force between 1998 and 2000. This may be attributed to the disconnection between the nature of SMEs and the way they are managed as well as to the wider societal context of the labour market (Jackson et al., 2008). This view suggests that SMEs in South Africa should better reflect the communities out of which they grow and foster employee commitment (Mbonyane and Ladzani, 2011). In addition, rather than focusing on financial rewards, SMEs should also consider other unconventional strategies to ensure employee job satisfaction, such as flexitime, shorter working hours and childcare provision to support employees with family commitments (Smit et al., 2005).

In addition, training and development seems to be another critical issue in South African SMEs. Horwitz (2013) and Van Scheers (2011) argue that training and development aims at changing attitudes and values, in the expectation that this will create a better understanding and tolerance among people from different societal, cultural and economic backgrounds. According to Rogerson (2009), entrepreneurs in South Africa believe that failures in SMEs are caused by a lack of managerial skills and training. Researchers contend to the view that most entrepreneurs in South Africa need targeted training aimed at developing essential entrepreneurial skills. Furthermore, research within the context of entrepreneurial development has shown that most SMEs in South Africa focus more on training, workshops and discussions on value sharing, racism and discrimination, and understanding different cultural norms (Rogerson, 2008). This approach within the context of HRM is regarded as the 'hard' approach. This 'hard' approach follows the assumption that meaningful change occurs through challenging existing organisational or institutional policies and employment practices (Horwitz et al., 1996). As such, entrepreneurs are gradually realising that there should be major changes in how they deploy their strategic resources to compete in the knowledge economy (Klapper et al., 2009). Therefore, enhancing the appropriate knowledge and skills through training and development is essential in ensuring that SMEs in South Africa enhance their competitiveness and contribute to economic development.

In summary, although there is not much empirical evidence on South African SMEs and the HR practices they use, there are aspects of HRM that can be identified. The main message from the available research is that there is a need for a greater emphasis on competitiveness, managerial skills and training, and retention strategies for skilled workers.

Ghana

Ghana, like many African countries, has gone through a number of socio-economic reforms since its independence in the year 1957. The philosophy of economic development since then can be summarised in the statement that government 'has a business to be in business' because the indigenous private sector could not be trusted to lead the economy to prosperity (Asante, 2000). The private sector in Ghana was therefore perceived as exploiting the poor (Prahalad, 2009). GDP in Ghana expanded 1.5% in the first quarter of 2018 over the previous quarter. GDP growth rate averaged 1.83% from 2006 until 2018, reaching an all-time high of 7.4% in 2011 and a record low of –2.2% in 2008 (Trading Economics, 2018). The country is getting closer to attaining a middle-income status by 2020, and the private sector is expected to play a leading role in this. The focus on private sector development has obvious implications for HRM practices, especially in SMEs where the dominant role of owners is observed (Kyereboah-Coleman and Biekpe, 2006).

Statistically speaking, SMEs account for about 92% of enterprises in Ghana, with 90% of all enterprises registered under the Registrar General's Office falling under the SME category (Abor and Quartey, 2010). The SME sector employs close to 70% of the Ghanaian labour force (Killick, 2010), caters for about 85% of manufacturing employment in Ghana (Abor and Quartey, 2010) and yet contributes only 6% to GDP. SMEs in Ghana fall into two major categories, namely urban enterprises and rural enterprises (Abor and Quartey, 2010). Between these two broad categories, some enterprises are well organised with registered offices and paid workers, while others are mainly made up of individual artisans and family enterprises without registered offices or paid workers, the latter normally being characteristic of rural enterprises.

The Ghanaian SME sector also consists of individual companies with self-employed persons who sometimes have unpaid family members assisting them, or trainees/apprentices who want to learn the job (Acquaah, 2011). These are categorised as microenterprises. Most of the rural enterprises belong to this category. There is also the small-sized enterprise group (up to 30 employees). There is also a third SME category, which is the medium-sized enterprises consisting of all firms that have between 30 and 100 employees (Abor and Quartey, 2010).

Mensah (2004) sums up the profiles of typical SMEs in Ghana. As he claims, they are, dominated by one person, with the owner-manager taking all major decisions. The entrepreneur possesses limited formal education and management skills are weak, thus inhibiting the development of a strategic plan for sustainable growth. Also, access to and use of new technologies, market information and access to credit from the banking sector are severely limited. Moreover, they experience extreme working capital volatility. Finally, the lack of technical expertise and inability to acquire skills and modern technology impede growth opportunities. The activities of SMEs in Ghana range from farming, agriculture, pottery and ceramics, carpentry, art and craft, textiles and garments, tourism, financial services, construction, food and food processing to manufacturing of spare parts and electronic assembling (Kayanula and Quartey, 2000).

HRM in SMEs in Ghana is mainly characterised by informality (Debrah, 2007) as in most emerging economies. In terms of recruitment and selection, the main responsibility belongs to top management, but interview panels can consist of managers from various levels within the organisation (Ofori and Aryeetey, 2011). The final decision to hire a candidate is usually made by top management, while for lower-level employees, the decision to hire is usually made by the person responsible for HR decisions (Ofori and Aryeetey, 2011). At another level, the lack of objectivity in recruitment and selection affects job analysis and HR planning. In Ghana, the instability in the political and economic environment makes it extremely difficult for SMEs to undertake any meaningful HR planning (Aryee, 2004). There is very limited HR planning as SMEs tend to be reactive rather than proactive. The reason is linked to the fact that SMEs lack organised HR departments and therefore lack adequate personnel with expertise in HRM (Ofori et al., 2012).

In most Ghanaian SMEs, although training is seen as an important HRM function, there are few opportunities for many employees to undergo training, particularly off-the-job external training (Abor and Quartey, 2010). Where there is some training, it is mainly informal on-the-job training. Few companies have their own well-structured internal training programmes. Even fewer have their own training schools. These schools cater to all employees, but it is usually lower- to mid-level employees that attend these schools (Quartey, 2012). Usually, top managers are sponsored for courses overseas or attend courses conducted by private training consultancy companies. The higher education institutions also play a significant role. They offer both undergraduate and postgraduate (e.g. MBA) degrees (Abor and Quartey, 2010). These institutions also offer courses in HRM and short post-experience courses to employees in the SME sector.

Reward or compensation strategies in SMEs for lower level, unskilled and semi-skilled employees are driven by the national minimum wage and determined through collective agreements (Kwenin et al., 2013). Where there is a union, wages are subject to negotiations (Debrah and Mmieh, 2009). Managerial salaries are also subject to individual negotiation, but any across-the-board annual increments are negotiated with their associations. In the absence of job evaluation, the main factor in wage determination is the ability of the organisation to pay. As jobs are hardly ever analysed or evaluated, the wage structures in most SMEs are a source of conflict, demotivation and dissatisfaction (Debrah and Mmieh, 2009).

Direct financial compensation for most employees in the Ghanaian SMEs is below the cost of living level (Agyapong, 2010). Thus, motivation essentially takes the form of financial and extrinsic compensation (salary, bonuses and fringe benefits). For example, it is common practice in Ghana to provide employees with accommodation or a rent allowance and to offer schemes covering health or medical expenses (Debrah and Mmieh, 2009). Some SMEs also provide a car allowance for senior employees. Currently, all allowances and other financial benefits are incorporated into the gross pay. With the abolition of the service benefit or gratuity in most SMEs in Ghana, workers rarely show a high degree of loyalty and commitment to the organisation (Agyemang and Ofei, 2013). In such an environment, individual rather than organisational goals drive employee behaviour.

Another HR function considered important by Ghanaian SME managers, but hardly ever linked to pay, is performance appraisals. Reward systems are not conditional upon performance or other organisation criteria (Appiah Fening et al., 2008). Perhaps this is linked to the low productivity of SMEs in Ghana. Performance appraisals are conducted annually, mainly for promotions or transfers, but rarely for compensation purposes (Abor and Biekpe, 2007; Abor and Quartey, 2010). Although performance appraisals are used to assess employees' training and developmental needs, many of these organisations usually do not have adequate resources to fill the training gaps. Finally, career planning, job design and personnel research are less developed in Ghanaian SMEs, although there is some evidence towards this direction (Ofori and Aryeetey, 2011).

In summary, there are some core HR practices applied by Ghanaian SMEs, such as recruitment, selection and training. Other HR activities, such as reward management, performance management, talent management and HR development, are considered as less developed, mainly due to their limited strategic purpose in SMEs.

Nigeria

Nigeria is home to more than 130 million people with 250 ethnic and religious groups and more than 500 spoken languages (Erondu et al., 2004). The main language of communication in Nigeria is English, but Hausa, Yoruba and Igbo are also widely used (Okpara, 2006).

Nigeria is considered as one of the emerging economies by the International Finance Corporation (2018). With an estimated population of 196 million in 2018 (World Population Review, 2018), Nigeria is the most populous country in Africa. Nigeria's population and potential natural and human resource base make it one of the most attractive countries for foreign investment in Africa.

The growth and development of HRM in Nigeria, as elsewhere in Sub-Saharan Africa, has undergone significant changes. In the traditional Nigerian societies, the armies and the administration of the kings, guilds, secret societies and other powerful social institutions had their own methods and procedures for selecting, inducting and training re-cruits to serve in various functions to ensure good governance of the society (Budhwar and Debrah, 2001). The start of colonialism, and with it, increased monetisation of the traditional economies, led to the importation of foreign organisations based on bureaucratic principles (Budhwar and Debrah, 2001). Employees were needed to work as mes-sengers, clerks, interpreters and labourers for the colonial administration and the emerging trading companies (Budhwar and Debrah, 2001), and this led to the HR function being one of the first areas to be addressed by British colonialists (Akinnusi, 1991).

Currently, HRM in Nigeria is influenced by strong cultural aspects. Azolukwam and Perkins (2009) support that HRM in Nigeria follows a hybrid approach that moves between local cultural peculiarities and normative pressures from Western-type HR management practices. Although most HR practitioners are open to HR (Azolukwam and Perkins, 2009), in the majority of Nigerian organisations, HRM is still underdeveloped, in that there are few formal HR departments, and where these exist, the focus is more around administrative functions (re-cruitment, payroll, record keeping) rather than strategic ones. In short, HRM in SMEs is still in its infancy (Fajana et al., 2011).

Paradoxically, HRM seems to be more strategic in SMEs and espe-cially in companies related to sectors such as oil, banking and consult-ing. Budhwar and Debrah (2001) argue that it is the owner-manager who carries out HR activities in SMEs, rather than formalised HR departments which make the HR approach more strategic. However, in Nigerian SMEs, there are usually no set policies or procedures (Ogunyomi and Bruning, 2016). As the company grows, the owner-manager may delegate HR tasks to an HR assistant. The HR manager may be a member of top management and typically reports to the head of finance and administration (Budhwar and Debrah, 2001).

As with other HRM functions, when discussing the recruitment and selection practices of Nigerian SMEs, a distinction must be made be-tween practices in SMEs on the one hand and in large organisations (including MNCs) on the other. As far as SMEs are concerned, vacancies are primarily filled through friends or relatives and through unsolicited applications (Budhwar and Debrah, 2001). Recruiting from universities used to be a common strategy; however, the declining market condi-tions and growth in unemployment have made this practice less popular (Okpara and Wynn, 2007). The use of consulting firms (headhunters) and media advertising is less common in SMEs (Chidi and Okpala, 2012). In terms of selection, aptitude and psychometric tests are increas-ing in popularity among organisations.

In short, Nigerian SMEs depict a mix of HRM formality and infor-mality depending on their industry. Historical and institutional factors have affected the presence of HRM practices in businesses, with some distinctive differences observed between SMEs and larger organisations. Overall, HRM in Nigerian SMEs seems to evolve between traditional aspects and normative pressures for modernisation mainly posed by Western MNCs.

Algeria

Algeria is one of the richest countries in North Africa because of its natural resources of arable land in the north and hydrocarbons (crude oil and natural gas) in the south (Budhwar and Debrah, 2001). Algeria is an emerging market attracting interest from companies around the world due to its large population (38 million), hydrocarbon wealth, expanding infrastructure needs and growing consumer product demand (US Department of State, 2014). Since the progressive adoption of a market economy in the 1990s, Algeria has witnessed growth in the SME sector, making this sector a major influencer of economic development and employment (Bouazza, 2015). Since then, successive governments have shown increasing efforts to support SMEs financially and upgrade their competitiveness (Mosbah and Debili, 2014). However, the Algerian economy has experienced shocks, primarily due to the sharp and sustained decline in oil prices since mid-2014 which led to large fiscal deficits and exacerbated an already weak fiscal position (International Monetary Fund, 2017).

Algerian SMEs employ no more than 250 people or have a total annual balance sheet not exceeding 500 million Algerian dinars (Mosbah and Debili, 2014). SMEs are the backbone of the private sector in Algeria. According to the Algerian Ministry of Industry, Algeria created an average of 60,000 SMEs per year in the 2012–2015 period (Oxford Business Group, 2018). The majority of SMEs are micro-sized enterprises. According to the Algerian national office of statistics (ONS), at the end of 2012, approximately 98% of all SMEs were microenterprises employing less than ten people. These statistics indicate that the Algerian economy heavily relies on microenterprises for absorbing unemployment on the one hand and creating wealth on the other hand (Bouazza, 2015). Algerian SMEs have a strong presence in the service sector (particularly transport), which accounts for nearly half of all SMEs, followed by other sectors, such as the building, construction, hydraulic, manufacturing, agriculture and energy sectors (Bouazza, 2015).

In terms of HRM practices, these are influenced by historical, cultural and institutional factors. HRM in Algeria is similar to many other emerging economies, but it has distinctive characteristics when considered in relation to other countries (Branine, 2006). According to Branine (2006), HRM in Algeria 'is intertwined with contradictory policies, practices and attitudes that have their origins in the cultural, historical, political and socio-economic developments of the country'

(p. 250). Historically speaking, the first directors to be appointed after independence in 1962 did not have any technical or managerial qualifications (Budhwar and Debrah, 2001). Half of the self-managed firms at that time did not have directors, just untrained substitute managers who had only completed an eight-week training course (Ottaway and Ottaway, 1970). Within this context, management practices, including HRM, were underdeveloped, although developments in HRM practice have taken place since then.

HRM in SMEs is semi-developed. In recruitment and selection, SMEs use key recruitment and selection tools, such as advertising jobs in newspapers, reviewing applications, holding interviews and testing candidates. However, many vacancies are filled through friends and relatives. Budhwar and Debrah (2001) note that the process of resourcing in Algeria is a bureaucratic and administrative formality; it is neither systematic nor objective. There have been many cases of vacancies being filled before the posts were advertised. It is normal for organisations to receive unsolicited and speculative applications. It is also common practice to hire new employees without necessarily having vacancies. The latter happens when friends and relatives apply for jobs. As a result, it is very often difficult to get employed without having contacts within the organisation (Amroune et al., 2014).

Acts of favouritism, nepotism or bribery are common and are summed up in the well-known Algerian SME concept of the 'Piston' (Branine, 2002). Application forms and documents which are not followed up through the use of the 'Piston' are often easily lost or ignored. The use of the 'Piston' to get jobs, goods and services easily has given many SME managers enhanced social prestige and strengthened their positions. Friendship and kinship can take precedence over qualifications and skills as managers feel obliged to support their relatives and friends (Branine, 2006). In return, the employees who get jobs through the 'Piston' feel obliged to those who hired them. Overall, recruitment is a bureaucratic process, requiring the applicant to gather various documents and complete numerous forms before they can submit their interest to the employer. The process is lengthy and often encounters delays due to missing documentation, while all applications and submitted documents are retained by employers (Budhwar and Debrah, 2001). However, if the 'Piston' is in action, qualifications required would be minimum required and the job would be offered directly. Budhwar and Debrah (2001) further discuss that Algerian employers place emphasis on a handwritten cover letter, although this does not mean that graphology is used as a selection tool. This is rather a practice inherited from the French bureaucracy.

Education and training are still heavily influenced by the French system in Algeria. A large number of French teachers and technical assistants continued to work in Algeria following its independence, and many Algerians still go to France to obtain further and higher education (Budhwar and Debrah, 2001). However, the educational system has not produced enough of a skilled labour force because the focus has been on general education and not on vocational education and training. There is a lack of awareness of the importance of continuous training in firms, and training is seen as a cost rather than an investment (Bouazza et al., 2015). The level of training varies from one organisation to another, even among SMEs in Algeria. There is a tendency to train some employees and not others and to use training as a reward for employees who may not need it (Budhwar and Debrah, 2001). Selection for training is rarely made on the basis of a training needs analysis or after a performance appraisal. Managerial judgement on who should and should not be on training programmes is the norm in Algerian SMEs.

Regarding employee rewards, a fixed monthly minimum wage guaranteed for all employees since 1978, and this is guaranteed for all employees, while the state's national income policy determines the grades and levels of payment in all sectors, including pay rises in state-owned enterprises (Budhwar and Debrah, 2001). Further to basic pay, the reward system in Algerian SMEs follows a Western trend (Mellahi and Frynas, 2003). These rewards include allowances, bonuses and a range of welfare provisions, such as sickness and disability allowances, old age pensions, family allowances and unemployment benefits, while managers enjoy enhanced benefits such as housing and travelling allowances (Budhwar and Debrah, 2001).

In summary, we can argue that there are strong historical, cultural and institutional elements affecting the application of HR practices in Algerian companies. The greatest effect is observed in recruitment and selection practices that are mainly influenced by networking and nepotism.

Summary

Chapter 4 explored HRM in SMEs in emerging economies located in Africa. The chapter particularly focused on South Africa, Ghana, Nigeria and Algeria. Not much empirical evidence was available on other African economies. SMEs in Africa are at the heart of employment expansion and are key to economic growth. Available research on South African SMEs discusses the need for a greater emphasis on competitiveness, managerial skills and training, and retention strategies for skilled workers. In Ghana, we found that SMEs apply some core HR practices, such as recruitment, selection and training. Other HR activities, such as reward management, performance management, talent management and HR development, are considered as less strategic. In Nigeria, SMEs depict a mix of HRM formality and informality depending on their industry. Historical and institutional factors have affected the presence of

HRM practices in businesses, with some distinctive differences observed between SMEs and larger organisations. Similarly, strong historical, cultural and institutional factors have shaped HRM application in SMEs in Algeria. The greatest effect is observed in recruitment and selection practices that are mainly influenced by networking and nepotism. The next chapter continues the exploration of HRM in SMEs in emerging economies by focusing on the Latin American region.

References

Abor, J. and Biekpe, N. (2007). Corporate governance, ownership structure and performance of SMEs in Ghana: Implications for financing opportunities. *Corporate Governance: The International Journal of Business in Society*, 7(3): pp. 288–300.

Abor, J. and Quartey, P. (2010). Issues in SME development in Ghana and South Africa. *International Research Journal of Finance and Economics*, 39(6): pp. 215–228.

Acquaah, M. (2011). Business strategy and competitive advantage in family businesses in Ghana: The role of social networking relationships. *Journal of Developmental Entrepreneurship*, 16(1): pp. 103–126.

Agyapong, D. (2010). Micro, small and medium enterprises' activities, income level and poverty reduction in Ghana – A synthesis of related literature. *International Journal of Business and Management*, 5(12): p. 196.

Agyemang, C. B. and Ofei, S. B. (2013). Employee work engagement and organisational commitment: A comparative study of private and public sector organisations in Ghana. *European Journal of Business and Innovation Research*, 1(4): pp. 20–33.

Akinnusi, D. M. (1991). Personnel management in Africa: A comparative analysis of Ghana, Kenya and Nigeria. In C. Brewster and S. Tyson, eds., *International Comparisons in Human Resource Management*. London: Pitman, pp. 159–172.

Amroune, B., Hafsi, T., Bernard, P. and Plaisent, M. (2014). 11 SMEs in developing countries and institutional challenges in turbulent environments: The case of Algeria. In E. V. Chrysostome and R. Molz, eds., *Building Businesses in Emerging and Developing Countries: Challenges and Opportunities*. London: Routledge: p. 215.

Appiah Fening, F., Pesakovic, G. and Amaria, P. (2008). Relationship between quality management practices and the performance of small and medium size enterprises (SMEs) in Ghana. *International Journal of Quality and Reliability Management*, 25(7): pp. 694–708.

Aryee, S. (2004). HRM in Ghana. In N. K. Kamoche, Y. A. Debrah, F. M. Horwitz and G. N. Muuka, eds., *Managing Human Resources in Africa*. London: Routledge, pp. 138–151.

Asante, Y. (2000). *Determinants of Private Sector Investment Behaviour in Ghana*. Legon: University of Ghana.

Azolukwam, V. A. and Perkins, S. J. (2009). Managerial perspectives on HRM in Nigeria: Evolving hybridisation? *Cross Cultural Management: An International Journal*, 16(1): pp. 62–82.

Bouazza, A. B. (2015). Small and medium enterprises as an effective sector for economic development and employment creation in Algeria. *International Journal of Economics, Commerce and Management*, 3(2): pp. 1–16.

Bouazza, A. B., Ardjouman, D. and Abada, O. (2015). Establishing the factors affecting the growth of small and medium-sized enterprises in Algeria. *American International Journal of Social Science*, 4(2): pp. 101–115.

Bowmaker-Falconer, A. and Day, G. (1995). *Human resources information and organisational effectiveness*, (unpublished paper). Graduate School of Business, University of Cape Town, pp. 1–8.

Bowmaker-Falconer, A., Horwitz, F. M., Jain, H. and Tagar, S. (1998). Employment equality programmes in South Africa: Current trends. *Industrial Relations Journal*, 29(3): pp. 222–233.

Branine, M. (2002). Algeria's employment policies and practice: An overview. *International journal of employment studies*, 10(1): p. 133.

Branine, M. (2006). Human resource management in Algeria. In P. S. Budhwar and K. Mellahi, eds., *Managing Human Resources in the Middle East*. London: Routledge, pp. 268–290.

Budhwar, P. S. and Debrah, Y. A. (2001). *Human Resources in Developing Countries*. Oxon: Routledge.

Chidi, C. O. and Okpala, O. P. (2012). Human capital resourcing practices and organisational performance: A study of selected organisations in Lagos State, Nigeria. In Azcarate A. L. V., ed., *Theoretical and Methodological Approaches to Social Sciences and Knowledge Management* [online]. Available from: https://www.intechopen.com/books/theoretical-and-methodological-approaches-to-social-sciences-and-knowledge-management. [Accessed 1 November 2018].

Debrah, Y. A. (2007). Promoting the informal sector as a source of gainful employment in developing countries: Insights from Ghana. *The International Journal of Human Resource Management*, 18(6): pp. 1063–1084.

Debrah, Y. A. and Mmieh, F. (2009). Employment relations in small- and medium-sized enterprises: Insights from Ghana. *The International Journal of Human Resource Management*, 20(7): pp. 1554–1575.

Erondu, E., Sharland, A. and Okpara, J. O. (2004). Corporate ethics in Nigeria: A test of the concept of an ethical climate. *Journal of Business Ethics*, 51(4): pp. 349–354.

Fajana, S., Owoyemi, O., Elegbede, T. and Gbajumo-Sheriff, M. (2011). Human resource management practices in Nigeria. *Journal of Management and Strategy*, 2(2): p. 57.

Fatoki, O. O. and Asah, F. (2011). The impact of firm and entrepreneurial characteristics on access to debt finance by SMEs in King Williams' Town, South Africa. *International Journal of Business and Management*, 6(8): p. 170.

Horwitz, F. M. (2013). Human resource management in Southern African multinational firms: Considering an Afro-Asian nexus. *Effective People Management in Africa*, 2: p. 126.

Horwitz, F. M., Bowmaker-Falconer, A. and Searll, P. (1996). Human resource development and managing diversity in South Africa. *International Journal of Manpower*, 17(4/5): pp. 134–151.

International Finance Corporation (2018). *IFC: The first six decades – Leading the way in private sector development.* (2nd edition). World Bank Group. [online]. Available at: www.ifc.org/wps/wcm/connect/6285ad53-0f92-48f1-ac6e-0e939952e1f3/IFC-History-Book-Second-Edition.pdf?MOD=AJPERES. [Accessed 1 September 2018].

International Monetary Fund (2017). *Algeria: selected issues.* [online]. Available at: www.imf.org/en/Publications/CR/Issues/2017/06/01/Algeria-Selected-Issues-44961. [Accessed 1 September 2018].

Jackson, T., Amaeshi, K. and Yavuz, S. (2008). Untangling African indigenous management: Multiple influences on the success of SMEs in Kenya. *Journal of World Business*, 43(4): pp. 400–416.

Kayanula, D. and Quartey, P. (2000). *The Policy Environment for Promoting Small- and Medium Sized Enterprises in Ghana and Malawi. Finance and Development Research Programme, Working Paper Series, 15.* Manchester: Institute for Development Policy and Management, University of Manchester.

Killick, T. (2010). *Development Economics in Action Second Edition: A Study of Economic Policies in Ghana.* Oxon: Routledge.

Klapper, L., Lewin, A. and Delgado, J. M. Q. (2009). *The Impact of the Business Environment on the Business Creation Process.*

Kwenin, D. O., Muathe, S. and Nzulwa, R. (2013). The influence of employee rewards, human resource policies and job satisfaction on the retention of employees in Vodafone Ghana Limited. *European Journal of Business and Management*, 5(12): pp. 13–20.

Kyereboah-Coleman, A. and Biekpe, N. (2006). The link between corporate governance and performance of the non-traditional export sector: Evidence from Ghana. *Corporate Governance: The International Journal of Business in Society*, 6(5): pp. 609–623.

Ladzani, W. M. and Van Vuuren, J. J. (2002). Entrepreneurship training for emerging SMEs in South Africa. *Journal of Small Business Management*, 40(2): pp. 154–161.

Long, C. S., Ajagbe, M. A. and Kowang, T. O. (2014). Addressing the issues on employees' turnover intention in the perspective of HRM practices in SME. *Procedia-Social and Behavioral Sciences*, 129: pp. 99–104.

Mbonyane, B. and Ladzani, W. (2011). Factors that hinder the growth of small businesses in South African townships. *European Business Review*, 23(6): pp. 550–560.

Mellahi, K. and Frynas, J. G. (2003). An exploratory study into the applicability of Western HRM practices in developing countries: An Algerian case study. *International Journal of Commerce and Management*, 13(1): pp. 61–80.

Mensah, S. (2004). *A review of SMEs financing schemes in Ghana.* UNIDO Regional Workshop for financing small and medium scale enterprises, pp. 1–20.

Mosbah, A. and Debili, R. (2014). Development of Algerian SMEs in the age of globalisation. *Journal of Business and Social Development*, 2(1): pp. 37–48.

Ofori, D. F. and Aryeetey, M. (2011). Recruitment and selection practices in small and medium enterprises: Perspectives from Ghana. *International Journal of Business Administration*, 2(3): p. 45.

Ofori, D. F., Sekyere-Abankwa, V. and Borquaye, D. B. (2012). Perceptions of the human resource management function among professionals: A Ghanaian study. *International Journal of Business and Management*, 7(5): p. 159.

Ogunyomi, P. and Bruning, N. S. (2016). Human resource management and organisational performance of small and medium enterprises (SMEs) in Nigeria. *The International Journal of Human Resource Management*, 27(6): pp. 612–634.

Okpara, J. O. (2006). The impact of personal characteristics on the job satisfaction of public sector managers in a developing economy: Implications for personnel development. *African Journal of Economics and Business Research*, 1(1): pp. 10–29.

Okpara, J. O. and Wynn, P. (2007). Human resource management practices in a transition economy: Challenges and prospects. *Management Research News*, 31(1): pp. 57–76.

Olawale, F. and Garwe, D. (2010). Obstacles to the growth of new SMEs in South Africa: A principal component analysis approach. *African Journal of Business Management*, 4(5): pp. 729–738.

Ottaway, D. and Ottaway, M. (1970). *Algeria: The Politics of a Socialist Revolution*. Berkeley: University of California Press.

Oxford Business Group (2018). *SMEs drive growth in non-energy sectors of the Algerian economy.* [online]. Available at: https://oxfordbusinessgroup.com/analysis/strength-numbers-through-increasingly-supportive-frameworks-small-and-medium-sized-enterprises-are. [Accessed 1 September 2018].

Prahalad, C. K. (2009). *The Fortune at the Bottom of the Pyramid: Eradicating Poverty Through Profits*. Upper Saddle River, NJ: Wharton School Publishing.

Quartey, S. H. (2012). Effect of employee training on the perceived organisational performance: A case study of the print-media industry in Ghana. *Human Resource Management (HRM)*, 4(15): pp. 77–87.

Rogerson, C. M. (2008). Tracking SMME development in South Africa: Issues of finance, training and the regulatory environment. *Urban Forum*, 19(1): pp. 61–81.

Rogerson, C. M. (2009). *Strategic review of local economic development in South Africa.* Final report submitted to Minister Sicelo Shiceka, Department of Planning and Local Government (DPLG). Commissioned by the DPLG and Afrikaanse Handelsinstituut (AHI). Supported by the Strengthening Local Governance Programme of GTZ.

Sakar, S. (2007). Labour history in India and South Africa: Some affinities and contrasts. *African Studies*, 66(2–3): pp. 181–200.

Smit, E., De Coning, T. J. and Visser, D. J. (2005). The relationship between the characteristics of the transformational leader and the entrepreneur in South African SMEs. *South African Journal of Business Management*, 36(3): pp. 51–63.

Smit, Y. and Watkins, J. A. (2012). A literature review of small and medium enterprises (SME) risk management practices in South Africa. *African Journal of Business Management*, 6(21): pp. 6324–6330.

Trading Economics (2018). *Ghana: Economic Indicators.* [online]. Available at: https://tradingeconomics.com/ghana/indicators. [Accessed 1 November 2018].

US Department of State (2014). *Algeria – Diplomacy in action.* [online]. Available at: www.state.gov/documents/organization/228915.pdf. [Accessed 1 September 2018].

Van Scheers, L. (2011). SMEs' marketing skills challenges in South Africa. *African Journal of Business Management*, 5(13), pp. 5048–5056.

Vollgraaff, R. (2015). *Africa to add more to workforce in 2035 than world combined.* [online]. Available at: www.bloomberg.com/news/articles/2015-04-28/africa-s-labor-force-newcomers-to-exceed-world-by-2035-imf-says. [Accessed 1 September 2018].

World Economic Forum (2015). *Why SMEs are key to growth in Africa.* [online]. Available at: www.weforum.org/agenda/2015/08/why-smes-are-key-to-growth-in-africa/. [Accessed 1 September 2018].

World Population Review (2018). *Nigeria population 2018.* [online]. Available at: http://worldpopulationreview.com/countries/nigeria-population/. [Accessed 1 September 2018].

5 HRM in SMEs in Emerging Market Economies III – Latin America

Introduction

This is the last of three chapters examining HRM practices in SMEs operating in EMEs. The chapter explores the Latin America region. Although there is various research evidence regarding HRM in Latin America, provided mainly by Davila and Elvira (see Davila and Elvira, 2009; Davila and Elvira, 2012; Elvira and Davila, 2005; Elvira and Davila, 2007), there is very limited information about management and HRM practices in SMEs. Therefore, this chapter attempts to explore two countries, Chile and Colombia, for which we found reliable data.

Chile

According to the CIA World Fact Book (2018a), although Chile declared its independence in 1810, it did not achieve decisive victory over the Spanish until 1818. Chile defeated Peru and Bolivia in the War of the Pacific (1879–1883) to win its present northern regions. In the 1880s, the Chilean central government gained control over the central and southern regions inhabited by the Mapuche. After a series of elected governments, the three-year-old Marxist government of Salvador Allende was overthrown in 1973 by a military coup led by General Augusto Pinochet, who ruled until a democratically elected president was inaugurated in 1990. Since the 1980s, there has been consistency in economic policies leading to steady growth, reduced poverty rates and securing the country's commitment to democratic and representative government.

According to OECD (2018), the Chilean economy has significantly improved over the last decades, partly due to a stable macroeconomic framework, structural reforms (e.g. trade and investment liberalisation) and strong natural-resource sectors. However, progress has recently slowed due to low and stagnant productivity. The OECD (2018) highlights key priorities for Chile in order to strengthen productivity and investment: first, to raise incomes and well-being through the strengthening of skills and greater inclusion of women and low-skilled workers in the labour force; second, to increase the quality of education and training for the unemployed in order to reduce the segmentation of the labour market; and third, to support promising firms to grow, export and innovate through reforms and further simplification of trade and regulatory procedures.

According to the Chilean government and the Ministry of Economy, approximately 81% of formally established companies are micro-companies, 18% are SMEs, and only 1% are large organisations (Arrau and Medina, 2014). SMEs account for the overwhelming majority of the total number of enterprises. In 2014, 98.5% of all enterprises were classified as SMEs, including employer and non-employer firms in all industries (OECD, 2016). As a result, the government places emphasis on SMEs given the sector's role in employment, and the possibility of improving its integration into the national economy and export-oriented production and marketing chains (World Bank, 2004).

Looking into HRM practices in Chile, one can say that the concept of managing people is less developed and, therefore, less integrated in organisations. This is associated with the unique cultural and historical aspects that seem to affect the way that HRM is deployed in organisations. According to Perez et al. (2012), HRM arrived in Chile in the 1980s due to the political transformation from a dictatorship to a liberal democracy. Chilean organisations needed to adapt to institutional pressures rooted in the demands of an international capitalistic market and become competitive. In these terms, they needed to adopt modern people management practices, like HRM, abandoning their personnel management systems (Bello-Pintado, 2015; Perez et al., 2012). This, in combination with the Chilean labour culture, which was dominated by authoritarian, individualistic, fatalistic, and legalistic norms, created a rather hostile environment for proper HRM adoption (Bickford, 2002).

In a similar vein, Rodriguez and Gomez (2009) argue that HRM in Chile does not include strategic activities and that it is rather based on administrative functions and pressure exerted by managers. They claim that that there are three distinct cultural in Chilean organisations, namely pessimistic/fatalistic, optimistic/maniac and pragmatic/bureaucratic, that determine people management practices. Moreover, a similar study by Rodriguez (2010) claimed that HRM practices in Chile follow the normative perspective of HRM, which implies that HRM practices should place direct control over employees' behaviour and performance. A more recent study by Rodriguez and Stewart (2017) confirms that HR practices follow specific historical and cultural norms in Chile that mainly illustrate the paternalistic nature of HRM that seems to dominate over most of the Chilean companies and public sector organisations.

This situation seems to be reflected in SMEs as well. HRM in Chilean SMEs is generally informal and of low priority, even though SMEs are labour-intensive organisations and HRM practices can help them improve their performance (Sels et al., 2006). On the one hand, the advantages of HRM in SMEs are the improvement of adaptation capacity and performance, talent attraction and retention, commitment, organisational effectiveness, and long-term growth and sustainability of qualified workers (Barrett and Mayson, 2006; Brand and Bax, 2002; Cardon and Steven, 2004). On the other hand, the negative consequences of less sophisticated HRM include unfair layoffs, reduced work stability, lack of qualified work, insufficient recruitment practices, scarce training, absence of performance assessment, and minimal application of equal opportunity policies (Bacon and Hoque, 2005).

The study by Rodriguez and Gomez (2009) mentioned earlier provides a good overview of the role of HRM in Chilean SMEs. They found that managers exerted great pressure on employees, that organisational efficiency was seen in isolation from HRM practices, that worker autonomy and empowerment were non-existent, and that managers placed emphasis on loyalty, dedication, compliance and professionalism as desired qualities in workers. In addition, they found that national and organisational culture have a significant impact on HRM practices in SMEs. In the majority of SMEs, a pessimistic/fatalistic paradigm dominated employment relations. They describe this paradigm as characterised by strong mechanisms of control and punishment, close supervision and control, no worker participation in decision-making, a leadership style exerted by means of orders, no mechanisms enabling workers to train or develop themselves and an arbitrary distribution of rewards.

In recruiting and selecting workers, posts are advertised using different means. Newspaper advertisements are the most common, although the use of the Internet has become increasingly popular. However, informal advertising via known associates, such as friends and family, is popular in Chile. As highlighted by Vargas and Paillacar (2000) in their exploratory study of fruit exporting organisations of the Central Valley, recruitment is very informal and mostly dominated by recommendations from friends and family. Given the strong stratification in Chilean society and the dominance of specific family groups, links through known associates are mostly common (Rodriguez, 2010). Friends and family operate under the umbrella of group preservation, which is common in collectivist societies (Hofstede, 1990).

In terms of selection practices, Rodriguez (2010) explains that these include interviews, role playing, teamwork and work-based scenario exercises, although these are in place only to 'fill out the paperwork'. She further explains that selection decisions are strongly determined by each candidate's 'pedigree' – who they know, with whom they associated, who recommended them and the degree of power of the person who recommended them. This is why personal references and recommendations are widely used as a selection tool by SMEs (Rodriguez, 2010). Recommendations also form part of the favour loyalty system (Gomez and Rodriguez, 2006), a way of cashing in on favours or returning favours.

Direct discrimination is present in recruitment and selection processes in Chilean SMEs. For example, Rodriguez (2010) explains that job adverts specify candidates falling within specific age groups and having specific characteristics (e.g. young, female, male, etc.). This results in ageist practices in the workplace. She concludes that, although qualifications are relevant in the selection process in Chilean SMEs, aspects such as the applicant's socio-economic background, physical appearance and educational background are all factors fostering discrimination at work. Indeed, earlier work by Abarca et al. (1998) suggests that appearance, age and gender differences are correlated with social status and create negative categories of difference leading to discrimination. Such practices are culturally embedded and have now been normalised into everyday business practice.

As far as training is concerned, it is not widely present in SMEs in Chile. Training opportunities are unplanned and generally follow trends in the market in terms of what seems popular rather than the result of learning and development strategies or HR planning (Robertson, 2003). For instance, participation in training is often determined by line managers with no input from workers or employees. Earlier work by Montero (1997) showed that training is regarded as an award given to employees by line managers. The employees receiving the training are seen as line managers' 'closest allies', 'friends/buddies' or 'right-hand people'. In this sense, the understanding of training as a reward is reinforced as something that these organisations give to 'deserving' workers. Internal events, such as IT training, teamwork and other forms of activities, are thought of by management as helpful in improving productivity (Montero, 1997). These are usually facilitated by both internal and external tutors and organised both on the job and off the job. In cases where events are planned during working hours, many participants report having to make up the hours used, which discourages them from requesting these opportunities.

In compensation and wages, pay scales are available neither to prospective nor to current employees. Information on pay scales is not provided to applicants; instead, applicants are asked to indicate their pay expectations, which are then discussed if called in for an interview (Lind et al., 2000). SMEs provide vague employee monetary rewards that are limited to statements such as 'competitive salary', 'salary according to experience' and 'salary according to market' with no indication of ranges (Rodriguez, 2010). In some SMEs, managerial salaries are not publicly available, and this generates tensions between staff. Also, applicants do not receive a formal written document stating their salary or any information about pay before or during the recruitment process (Goldberg and Palladini, 2008). Moreover, when applying for work in SMEs, applicants use friends and acquaintances to find out the typical salary associated with the post they are applying to. When asked about their preferred salary by recruiters, they indicate a lesser amount in order to increase their chance of being shortlisted (Goldberg and Palladini, 2008).

This practice raises questions of fairness as it is unclear to employees what others in similar posts are earning. Composition of wages in SMEs is said to be related to productivity. Nonetheless, Rodriguez (2010) mentions that most wages do not reward productivity but rather seniority (over base salary) and provide increases in work intensity (through commissions, production bonuses and treats). This distinction is relevant because it leads to a mixed wage system (a basic component plus a variable component). The basic component is very low, and the variable component is 'where the real money is', as their final wage increases through commissions obtained when reaching higher targets. Consequently, productivity and work intensity are for practical reasons, one and the same as an increase in work intensity is linked to monetary rewards for higher productivity levels (Rodriguez, 2010).

In terms of performance evaluation, there is a lack of credibility of performance appraisal systems in Chilean SMEs which has been documented in the earlier work of Koljatic and Rosene (1993). According to this study, SME managers value them as a means for acknowledging and rewarding performance. On the contrary, employees perceive performance appraisals as a tick-box exercise. Some employees do not participate in performance appraisals, while some others have formal appraisals where they discuss with their line manager/supervisor their workload, accomplishments, improvements needed, targets for the next period and document all these discussions (Koljatic and Rosene, 1993). Overall, performance appraisals do not have a developmental dimension but are rather seen as a formality (Rodriguez, 2010). The perception is that performance is achieved by telling employees what needs to be done, by expecting high performance and by threatening with possible dismissals when performance is poor.

Finally, worker participation in SMEs has been historically controversial. Employee relations have traditionally followed the pattern of the 'Hacienda' (Rodriguez et al., 2005), where employers hold and exercise power, while workers are expected to show loyalty to superiors. Employee voice is limited due to fear of repercussion (being punished, ostracised or dismissed), while unionisation has significantly decreased over time (Rodriguez and Gomez, 2009). Work relationships are based on authority, and there is an expectation that workers listen and do as they are told with no possibility for workers to voice out their problems (Espinosa and Morris, 2002). The hierarchical and formal structure of relationships in SMEs is also highlighted as an aggravating factor. Rodriguez (2010) discusses how line managers are perceived as strict, arrogant and indifferent, with management styles that prioritise results over processes and people. They believe that workers do little to engage, take advantage of situations, show no initiative and do not invest effort at work.

In summary, HR practices in SMEs in Chile are primarily informal. There are cultural, historical and institutional elements that prohibit small companies from following more modern management practices. In recruitment, SMEs use formal technical criteria for recruitment and selection complemented by informal references and recommendations from individuals linked to the organisation through friendship or kinship. Direct discrimination is also quite common. Training is not widely present in SMEs, and where this takes place, it is line managers who decide which employee will receive it. Mixed reward systems are implemented, using a basic component and a variable component, but the focus is on seniority and not productivity. Performance appraisals lack credibility and voice at work is significantly restricted.

Colombia

According to the CIA World Fact Book (2018b), Colombia was one of the three countries that emerged after the dissolution of Gran Colombia in 1830 (the others were Ecuador and Venezuela). During the 1990s, a long-term conflict between government forces, paramilitaries and anti-government groups escalated. The Colombian government signed a final peace accord with the Revolutionary Armed Forces (FARC) in 2016, which was subsequently ratified by the Colombian Congress. The accord committed FARC to demobilise, disarm and reincorporate into society and politics. It also committed the Colombian government to create three new institutions: a truth commission, a special unit to coordinate the search for those who disappeared during the conflict, and a 'Special Jurisdiction for Peace' to administer justice for conflict-related crimes. Despite the long period of internal conflict, Colombia has developed strong institutions characterised by peaceful and transparent elections and by the protection of civil liberties (Rodrik, 2000).

In the legal definition of SMEs in Colombia (Law 590/2000, amended by Law 905/2004), small firms are defined as those with 11–50 employee and assets of 501–5,000 legal minimum monthly salaries (around US$0.1–1.1 million), while medium-sized firms are those with 51–200 employees and assets of 5,001–30,000 legal minimum monthly salaries (around US$1.1–6.7 million) (Stephanou and Rodriguez, 2008). The 1991 Constitution acknowledges that a competent civil service is key to development, and for this reason, the reforms introduced also focus on HRM as a key priority to a good governance agenda (OECD, 2013). There is, therefore, a growing knowledge around HRM practices in Colombian organisations influencing practices in SMEs (Castrogiovanni et al., 2011).

HRM in Colombian SMEs moves along formal and informal aspects. There is some research evidence about a few HR practices applied in SMEs in Colombia. Employee training and development do not seem to have achieved a level of strategic development in Colombian SMEs (Pastrana and Sriramesh, 2014). Even though employee training was part of the survival strategy and corporate competition during moments of crisis, it was still not oriented towards intellectual capital or explicit knowledge management in the majority of these SME companies. For SMEs in Colombia, training and development concentrate on two approaches: quality and competency management (Batra and Tan, 2003). In nearly all economic sectors, the quality approach comes from the implementation of the ISO 9000 certification, which is one of the requirements for contracting services or providing goods and one of the most important forms of company recognition (Vásquez-Bernal and Mosquera-Laverde, 2018). In addition, Osorio and Higuera (2018) discuss that lifelong learning is a government priority, so emphasis is placed on increasing formal education, as well as educational attainment through informal education. Their research found that large firms in Colombia are more likely to provide training than SMEs, while newer firms more often use training in relation to older firms. The majority of firms offer on-the-job training, rather than off-the-job methods like seminars (Osorio and Higuera, 2018), with approximately 72% of training conducted at work (Ogliastri et al., 2009). In some SMEs, training is conducted by experienced employees. Lucero and Spinel (2002) affirm that this is more frequent in the service sector than in the manufacturing sector and in companies with over 100 employees. According to their work, service companies and medium-sized companies decide on training needs without consulting line managers or employees, while training is frequently reactive and unplanned. Where training needs are planned, these are often determined by surveys, performance evaluations, 360-degree evaluations and employee competency development plans. Areas of training and development include change management, succession planning, individual development and skills training (Ogliastri et al., 2009).

Regarding compensation, research by Davila and Elvira (2009) on Latin America has found that remuneration in Colombian SMEs is personalised to a great degree, especially in the top organisational levels. Their work has also found that, at the worker level, remuneration is set according to the legal minimum salary, which is subject to annual negotiation between the government and the labour unions. Any salary increases are negotiated independently by each company according to the Colombian labour and union system, and based on the legal and extralegal benefits agreed upon in the past. Variable compensation (compensation according to sales volume) based on results is a frequently used reward strategy in sales and at executive levels in Colombian SMEs (Davila and Elvira, 2009). Fixed compensation is offered in 40% of cases, flexible compensation in 35% and variable compensation in 25% of cases (Dinero, 2003).

Compensation structures in Colombia have experienced change, particularly after the 1997 Colombian economic crisis. Davila and Elvira (2009) discuss how businesses moved from fixed compensation plans to payment structures based on results and performance, not simply seniority. At the same time, performance management is perceived as problematic as it is frequently used to determine salary increases without any real impact on employee productivity or performance.

Compensation in Colombian SMEs is complex and with great inequities and disparities (Ruiz, 2002). Work by Ogliastri et al. (2009) found that it is common to observe differences of 50–100 times between the maximum and minimum salaries in the same SME organisation. Gender discrimination in terms of salary and hierarchical levels is also observable because there are more men than women in high positions. These imbalances are more frequent in the private sector, particularly in smaller enterprises, than in the public sector or large organisations. These observations indicate to a paternalistic cultural behaviour with an absence of rational strategies for managing employee compensation (Ogliastri et al., 2009).

In short, Colombian organisations struggle between formality and informality of HRM. Public organisations have more formalised HR practices, while formalisation in SMEs seems to stem from laws and regulations organisations need to abide by. The overall state of HRM can be considered underdeveloped, and more research is needed to understand various aspects of HRM practice and application in SMEs.

Summary

Chapter 5 focused on EMEs in Latin American EMEs, particularly on the role of SMEs and HRM in the Chilean and Colombian contexts. We focused on these two countries only, since there is limited reliable evidence about HRM in SMEs in other countries. Although there is a group of scholars investigating HRM in Latin American countries, their work seems to focus mainly on large corporations. From our analysis, we can argue that HRM in SMEs in these two Latin American emerging markets is undergoing evolvement. This evolvement process is determined by historical, cultural and institutional factors. HRM logics are moving around particular historical developments in both countries with their transition of their political regimes. In addition, strong institutional influences, like globalised market demands, press companies to modernise their management practices, including HRM practices. However, specific cultural aspects seem to have a substantial impact on HRM application in small and medium companies. For example, the authoritarian cultural aspect that seems to be dominant in many Latin American countries (including the two explored in this chapter) also seems to define working relationships in general and HRM practices in particular. In other words, the implementation of modern people management practices depends heavily on top management, which has the legitimate authority to reinforce HRM application.

Conclusions for EMEs

Chapters 3–5 explored the application of HRM in SMEs in EMEs. We focused on a selection of emerging economies from each region for which some research was available. The discussion in these chapters showed that HRM in SMEs is moving between two aspects. First, there are both strong cultural and institutional features influencing HR adoption. For example, concepts such as the 'Guanxi' in China and the 'Piston' in Algeria dominate over HR practices like recruitment, selection, performance appraisal and sometimes career development. At the same time, there are strong institutional factors that influence HR adoption in SMEs in EMEs. For instance, in some countries, like Ghana, Vietnam, South Korea, Nigeria and Colombia, there are either government pressures to follow specific HR practices or pressures from large companies, mainly MNCs, that enhance (and sometimes demand) specific HR practices of local partner SMEs. The second aspect relates to formality versus informality. In particular, it seems that SMEs in EMEs are moving between formality and informality of HR practices based on their organisational contexts. For example, companies in the manufacturing industry seem to be keener to adopt formal HR strategies.

References

Abarca, N., Majluf, N. and Rodríguez, D. (1998). Identifying management in Chile: A behavioural approach. *International Studies of Management and Organisation*, 28(2): pp. 18–37.

Arrau, P. G. and Medina, F. M. (2014). Human resource management in small and medium-sized vineyards in Chile. *Agricultural Economics*, 41(2): pp. 141–151.

Bacon, N. and Hoque, K. (2005). HRM in the SME sector: Valuable employees and coercive networks. *International Journal of Human Resources Management*, 16(11): pp. 1976–1999.

Barrett, R. and Mayson, S. (2006). Exploring the intersection of HRM and entrepreneurship – Guest editors' introduction to the special edition on HRM and entrepreneurship. *Human Resource Management Review*, 16: pp. 443–446.

Batra, G. and Tan, H. (2003). SME technical efficiency and its correlates: Cross-national evidence and policy implications. *World Bank Institute Working Paper*, 9.

Bello-Pintado, A. (2015). Bundles of HRM practices and performance: Empirical evidence from a Latin American context. *Human Resource Management Journal*, 25(3): pp. 311–330.

Bickford, L. N. (2002). Preserving memory: The past and the human rights movement in Chile. *Democracy and Human Rights in Latin America*, 21(6): pp. 9–30.

Brand, M. and Bax, E. (2002). Strategic HRM for SMEs: Implications for firms and policy. *Education Training Journal*, 44(8): pp. 451–463.

Cardon, M. and Stevens, C. E. (2004). Managing human resources in small organizations: What do we know? *Human Resources Management Review*, 14(3): pp. 295–323.

Castrogiovanni, G. J., Urbano, D. and Loras, J. (2011). Linking corporate entrepreneurship and human resource management in SMEs. *International Journal of Manpower*, 32(1): pp. 34–47.

CIA World Fact Book (2018a). *South America: Chile*. [online]. Available at: www.cia.gov/library/publications/the-world-factbook/geos/ci.html. [Accessed 1 September 2018].

CIA World Fact Book (2018b). *South America: Colombia*. [online]. Available at: www.cia.gov/library/publications/the-world-factbook/geos/co.html. [Accessed 1 September 2018].

Davila, A. and Elvira, M. M. (2009). *Best Human Resource Management Practices in Latin America*. Oxford: Routledge.

Davila, A. and Elvira, M. M. (2012). Latin American HRM models. In C. Brewster and W. Mayrhofer, eds., *Handbook of Research on Comparative Human Resource Management*. Cheltenham: Edward Elgar, pp. 478–493.

Dinero (2003). *Gestión del talento. Las seis claves del éxito* [Talent management. The six keys to success], 188: p. 34.

Elvira, M. M. and Davila, A. (2005). Emergent directions for human resource management research in Latin America. *The International Journal of Human Resource Management*, 16(12): pp. 2265–2282.

Elvira, M. M. and Davila, A. (2007). *Managing Human Resources in Latin America: An Agenda for International Leaders*. Oxford: Routledge.

Espinosa, M. and Morris, P. (2002). *Calidad de vida en el trabajo: Percepciones de los trabajadores. Cuadernos de Investigación No. 16*. Dirección del Trabajo, Chile. [online]. Available at: www.dt.gob.cl. [Accessed 25 April 2009].

Goldberg, M. and Palladini, E. (2008). *Chile: A Strategy to Promote Innovative Small and Medium Enterprises*. Washington, DC: The World Bank.

Gomez, C. F. and Rodriguez, J. K. (2006). Four approximations to Chilean culture: Authoritarianism, legalism, fatalism and compadrazgo. *Asian Journal of Latin American Studies*, 19(3): pp. 43–65.

Hofstede, G. (1990). *Cultures and Organisations: Software of the Mind*. London: McGraw Hill.

Koljatic, M. and Rosene, F. (1993). *La Administración de Recursos Humanos en Chile: Practicas y Percepciones*. Chile: Facultad de Ciencias Económicas y Administrativas, P. Universidad Católica de Chile.

Lind, P., Sepúlveda, E. and Nuñez, J. (2000). On the applicability of a computer model for business performance analysis in SMEs: A case study from Chile. *Information Technology for Development*, 9(1): pp. 33–44.

Lucero, P. M. and Spinel, F. (2002). *Estudio sobre la estructura y necesidades de capacitación en la corporación industrial "Las granjas" de Bogotá* [Study of the structure and necessities in the industrial corporation "Las granjas" in Bogotá], unpublished thesis in Business Administration, Universidad de los Andes, Bogotá.

Montero, C. (1997). *La revolución empresarial en Chile*. Santiago, Chile: Dolmen Ediciones.

OECD (2013). *Colombia: Implementing good governance*. [online]. Available at: https://read.oecd-ilibrary.org/governance/colombia-implementing-good-governance_9789264202177-en#page3. [Accessed 1 September 2018].

OECD (2016). *Financing SMEs and entrepreneurs 2016: An OECD scoreboard.* [online]. Available at: www.oecd-ilibrary.org/industry-and-services/financing-smes-and-entrepreneurs-2016/chile_fin_sme_ent-2016-11-en. [Accessed 1 September 2018].

OECD (2018). *OECD economic surveys: Chile 2018.* [online]. Available at: www.oecd-ilibrary.org/economics/oecd-economic-surveys-chile-2018_eco_surveys-chl-2018-en. [Accessed 1 September 2018].

Ogliastri, E., Ruiz, J. and Martinez, I. (2009). Human resource management in Colombia. In A. Davila and M. M. Elvira, eds., *Best Human Resource Management Practices in Latin America.* Oxon: Routledge, pp. 165–177.

Osorio, F. B. and Higuera, L. (2018). *The demand for training in Colombia and the lifelong learning project. DIFIF-WB collaboration on knowledge and skills in the new economy.* World Bank. [online]. Available at: http://siteresources.worldbank.org/EDUCATION/Resources/278200-1126210664195/1636971-1126210694253/Colombia_Case_Study.pdf. [Accessed 1 September 2018].

Pastrana, N. A. and Sriramesh, K. (2014). Corporate social responsibility: Perceptions and practices among SMEs in Colombia. *Public Relations Review,* 40(1): pp. 14–24.

Perez Arrau, G., Eades, E. and Wilson, J. (2012). Managing human resources in the Latin American context: The case of Chile. *The International Journal of Human Resource Management,* 23(15): pp. 3133–3150.

Robertson, P. L. (2003). The role of training and skilled labour in the success of SMEs in developing economies. *Education and Training,* 45(8/9): pp. 461–473.

Rodriguez, J. K. (2010). Employment relations in Chile: Evidence of HRM practices. *Relations Industrielles,* 65(3): pp. 424–446.

Rodriguez, J. K. and Gomez, C. F. (2009). HRM in Chile: The impact of organisational culture. *Employee Relations,* 31(3): pp. 276–294.

Rodriguez, J. K. and Stewart, P. (2017). HRM and work practices in Chile: The regulatory power of organisational culture. *Employee Relations,* 39(3): pp. 378–390.

Rodriguez, D., Rios, R., De Solminihac, E. and Rosene, F. (2005). Human resource management in Chile. In A. Davila and M. M. Elvira, eds., *Managing Human Resources in Latin America.* London: Routledge, pp. 149–164.

Rodrik, D. (2000). Institutions for high-quality growth: What they are and how to acquire them. *Studies in Comparative International Development,* 35(3): pp. 3–31.

Ruiz, G. J. (2002). *Nóminas de personal y demografía organizacional: Tres ejemplos de análisis* [Payroll of personnel and organisational demographics: Three examples of analysis], unpublished manuscript. School of Business Administration, Universidad de los Andes, Bogotá.

Sels, L., De Winne, S., Maes, J., Delmotte, J., Faems, D. and Forrier, A. (2006). Unravelling the HRM–Performance link: Value-creating and cost-increasing effects of small business HRM. *Journal of Management Studies,* 43(2): pp. 319–342.

Stephanou, C. and Rodriguez, C. (2008). *Bank financing to small and medium-sized enterprises (SMEs) in Colombia.* Policy Research Working Paper, No. 4481, The World Bank, Financial and Private Sector Development Unit.

Vargas, G. and Paillacar, R. (2000). Estrategias de reclutamiento y selección de recursos humanos en empresas frutícolas de la zona central de Chile: estudio exploratorio. *Ciencia e Investigación Agraria*, 27(3): pp. 169–180.

Vásquez-Bernal, O. A. and Mosquera-Laverde, W. E. (2018). Impact of integrated management systems on organisations and the impact of road projects on biodiversity in Colombia. *World Transactions on Engineering and Technology Education*, 16(1): pp. 47–53.

World Bank (2004). *Chile: A strategy to promote innovative small and medium enterprises. Report No. 29114*. [online]. Available at: http://documents. worldbank.org/curated/en/857791468022465115/pdf/291141Chile0St1e0S MEs01green0cover1.pdf. [Accessed 1 September 2018].

6 Transition Economies of Central and Eastern Europe

Introduction

Within the European periphery, a number of countries have been in a process of economic transition since the 1990s (Morley et al., 2009). Their transition relates to moving from centrally planned (socialist) economies to capitalist ones. The countries that used to belong either to the USSR block or to the Yugoslav state have undergone a set of structural transformations intended to develop market-based institutions and logics (Feige, 2017). They are well known as ex-communist or post-communist countries, and they have been classified as 'transition economies' (Stark and Bruszt, 1998). The main features of this transformation process can be summarised in the following aspects: removal of trade barriers; privatisation of state-owned enterprises; emergence of various businesses (mainly SMEs) founded on restructured, formerly collectively run enterprises and resources; and a development of a financial system entitled to support and facilitate macroeconomic stabilisation and private investments (Feige, 1991).

The ex-communist states are a test bed for many management concepts, including HRM ones. The socialist model of employee relations under which these countries were organised in the period before 1990 totally collapsed, leaving the field open to a major dilemma: should these states follow a carefully regulated, collaborative approach – act as coordinated market economies (CMEs) – or follow a regulation-free, competitive approach, typical of liberal market economies (LMEs)? Hall and Soskice (2001) argue that countries can be successful at either end of this spectrum, but mixed systems are much less likely to be successful. Beyond the dichotomous argument of CMEs and LMEs, it seems that this ideal model cannot explain the current state of these nonideal types of countries in Central and Eastern Europe (CEE) (Szamosi et al., 2010). In addition, it seems that different ex-communist states have made varying decisions about which model to follow (Psychogios et al., 2014).

Since the 1989 collapse of the Berlin Wall, a dramatic situation emerged for the lives of citizens in these countries due to the outcomes of the switch from centrally planned to market economies. Borders have opened for the free movement of capital, goods and labour. In these countries, economies and peoples' lives have changed considerably in a short period of time. However, while it is clear what they are transitioning *from*, it is not exactly clear what they are transitioning *to*. This seems to be the case for many SMEs operating within these economies. Most of them are very small. The process of liberalisation has increased foreign direct investments and led a number of MNCs to establish a presence in the region. MNCs are powerful, particularly in countries where systems and procedures are in flux, far from fully entrenched, and where governments are desperate for foreign investment (Psychogios et al., 2014). Their dominance, though, seems to influence, albeit not holistically, the operation of SMEs that try to modernise practices following Western management prototypes (Wood et al., 2012).

Nevertheless, the data available on post-communist CEE economies indicate that they need to be studied and treated separately (Whitley, 1999). These economies, as some scholars argue (Batt et al., 2009; Kuruvilla and Ranganathan, 2009), represent a new capitalist system. This system is not similar to other EMEs in various other places around the world, as we have seen in the previous chapters. Furthermore, what makes emerging European countries unique is that, in general, despite varying degrees of similarity, their individual economic performance and size differ substantially (Schwartz and McCann, 2007). These substantive differences have been brought to the forefront during the recent economic downturn with some of these countries being more susceptible to what has been occurring around them. Thus, it is important to understand the development of HRM and SMEs in these countries separately from other EMEs.

Developments of HRM in Central and Eastern European Economies

Psychogios and Wood (2010) suggest that there is little doubt about the fluctuating nature of HRM in CEE markets. To this, Michailova et al. (2009) argue that in juxtaposition to Western Europe, CEE integrates a variance in HR practices and policies. This is due to the various institutions that embed formal and informal rules; these mould behaviour both within and between work organisations and other social actors. For example, in post-communist countries of CEE, legal institutions are still in the developmental stage, and property rights are still relatively weak. In addition, the dominance of proportional representation electoral systems in many CEE countries makes the differentiation of countries within the region more difficult and complex to achieve (Pagano and Volpin, 2005). While there is little doubt that political ideologies of ruling parties play a part (Roe, 2003), what precisely constitutes the former and the latter in CEE reflects specific historical experiences, and the disproportionate power of external players, such as the incorrigibly neo-liberal International Monetary Fund (IMF). In other words, what may be objectively conceived as left- or right-wing may be somewhat different in the CEE region, while even left-wing parties have had little room for manoeuvre since the financial crisis.

While the post-communistic countries in CEE are generally lumped together into a broad transitional category, it is something of a truism to state that it has been an extremely protracted transition process, and that for many countries there is no visible end to this process (Lane, 2007). Some transitional countries have veered relatively close to the lib-eral market model (e.g. the Czech Republic and the Baltics) and two have gradually moved to the coordinated market model (the Eurozone states of Slovakia and Slovenia) (Lane, 2007). Yet others appear to have em-barked on a distinct trajectory, characterised by high levels of corruption, poor law enforcement, high inequality, the sustained impoverishment of many, yet with islands of economic activity (above all, those linked to the politically well-connected prospering) (Szamosi et al., 2010).

The intuitional differences along with the different progress of the capitalist process are also reflected in HRM development in these coun-tries. In particular, there are key variations in the capacity of national training systems, in the capacity of organised labour and in the relative importance of family ties in terms of issues such as resourcing (Szamosi et al., 2010). First, different HRM models are likely to be encountered not just in different places – for example, between the uneven regulatory context of Slovenia and the 'wild capitalism' of Serbia (Upchurch and Marinkovic, 2011) – but also in different firm types, such as between indigenous large firms, MNCs, and SMEs, mostly family-owned. Sec-ond, at best, national training systems have battled to keep up with the changing HR demands at the firm level, delivering outmoded skills and/ or overly costly training out of reach to many companies and individuals (Zupan and Kase, 2005). Third, careers have generally become more insecure: firms have become a lot more opportunistic in their planning, with a large component of the workforce becoming reconciled to insecure working and/or a high degree of job mobility (Roberts, 2001). Finally, voice mechanisms are often weak and ineffective. In post-communistic economies, many unions have battled to recapture legitimacy in the wake of a transmission belt role under the preceding order (Psychogios et al., 2014).

Research on management practices in larger organisations in the CEE region has shown that HRM practices are linked to the economic tran-sition from post-communist to premature capitalist systems (Psychogios et al., 2014; Tung and Lazarova, 2006) based on the notion of central bureaucratic control of employees, although there is some evidence of a move towards more flexible practices (Michailova et al., 2009). Some recent studies show strong evidence of formalisation of HRM, especially in SMEs operating in CEE economies. Bogicevic Milikic et al. (2008) argue that formalised HRM systems and policies are becoming institutionally accepted and that HRM systems in some post-communist countries have undergone transformation from systems focused primarily on an administrative-traditional approach (bureaucratic monitoring of procedures and maintaining personnel records) to more advanced systems with HRM having a key role in strategy, policy and operational HRM decision-making. Similarly, Psychogios et al. (2016) found that HRM in SMEs in post-communistic south-eastern European countries becomes more formal with the international expansion of the firm, as well as with organisation enlargement.

So where do things currently stand in terms of HRM in CEE economies? Brewster et al. (2010) observed that there is a 'black hole' of sorts related to HR research in the region and Szamosi et al. (2010) determined the same. Through this chapter, we try to shed more light on this less-explored phenomenon. The next sections attempt to analyse HRM in SMEs in some countries in this region.

Poland

Poland, like many Eastern European countries, was led through communist governance until relatively recent times. The movement away from communism has resulted in a rapid change in the organisational landscape, seeing a rise in privatisation of previously centralised industries. This has contributed to an increased number of SMEs. Another relevant chapter of recent Polish history is the entry into the EU in May 2004. This particular event led to an unprecedented level of immigration into Western Europe of approximately 2 million Polish nationals (OECD, 2018) of whom the majority was of working age. For Polish organisations, this had a monumental impact on the employment landscape, where approximately 5% of the population was left seeking work in other areas of Europe.

To build on this contextual information, an understanding of Polish culture can help understand the influences on organisational behaviour. The dimensions attributed to the Polish culture by Hofstede (2011) could be summarised in the statement that Poland is a hierarchical society. This can be attributed to its communist past with strong, hierarchical, centralised organisations. Having said that, Poland scores high in terms of individualism. In organisational terms, this reflects on an individualised relationship between employee and management, which also stretches to social aspects; each individual or family is responsible for looking after themselves. These conflicting aspects can be attributed to a culture shift where Poland started to move away from the mindset of a communist governance towards a more individualistic society. For SMEs, this could be an interesting area of research, especially as ageing senior figures in organisations, largely brought up through the communist post-war era, step down from leadership roles, allowing new, younger and individualist-minded leaders to step into their shoes. Moreover, Poland scores highly on the cultural aspect of uncertainty avoidance. This is very relevant to HRM practices in SMEs as it reflects a strong need for rules and high importance placed on hard work and reliability. This, on face value, could be deemed a positive element for Polish organisations whose work-force work within the constraints set by management. To complement the high uncertainty score, Polish culture reveals a low satisfaction from indulgence, showing little need for gratification and more short-term-oriented goals.

Beyond cultural aspects, there are specific institutional features that influence Polish systems overall and SMEs operation in particular. For example, corruption within Polish institutions has been noted by Bluhm and Schmidt (2008) as a destructive influence on SMEs, stating that it can lead to cutting costs on labour and to weakening of motivation to improve quality. The two authors also provide an account of how after the fall of communism, previously corrupt black-market products and finances were used to create new enterprises by well-educated, influential, previously communist organisational leaders. The World Bank (2013) identified that corruption in Poland is not satisfactorily tackled due to an unwillingness from political leaders to support anti-corruption cam-paigns leading to complacency at all levels of the state (Sutch et al., 1999). In addition, institutional aspects relate to powerful financial structures. During the dramatic changes of the early 1990s, multiple Western banks invested heavily in Poland and bought out many domestic banks. This was on a scale far beyond anything seen in Western Europe, with Poland receiving upwards of 67% foreign investment in the banking sector. The impact this had on SMEs was pivotal, as some Polish SMEs did not see the worth of Western influences. This resulted in a lack of funding that saw some industries fall into crisis. Following the move towards a market economy, there has also been an increase in MNCs operating within Poland. These MNCs, often with extreme levels of wealth in comparison with domestic Polish organisations, are dominating the Polish business system, putting local SMEs in a critical situation.

While somewhat sparse in comparison with Western cultures, some research has been conducted in the Polish SME sector to understand the HRM practices they undertake. The field of HRM research benefits from a balance between theoretical developments and practical, informative research from countries such as Poland. Polish SMEs have a tendency to invest in generic HRM practices, which are often lower in cost than be-spoke systems based on individual needs. Further to this, Maczynski and colleagues (2010) identified that little change has been witnessed in man-ager attitudes towards HRM practices since the formation of a market-based economy. It is suggested that behavioural elements of Polish SME leaders have been unaffected by political and economic change. One explanation of why this may be is that leaders are more likely to be older and, therefore, more accustomed and aligned to communist-based organisational ideologies. The later sections look at specific HRM practices across a variety of areas, including learning and development, talent management, performance management and employee engagement.

A study into Polish SMEs was undertaken by Struzyna and colleagues (2009) across 193 SME organisations, seeking responses from owners, managers and specialists. The findings show that, in a similar vein to many Western European SMEs, HRM practices are often informal, and this is attributed to financial costs associated with implementing and maintaining them. The research also suggests that Polish SMEs more often than not seek to practice within their statutory and legal obligations, but rarely seek anything in addition to the minimum expected. In addition to this, specific quantitative data is provided on the prevalence of certain HRM practices making for interesting reading, especially as data of a similar nature is lacking elsewhere. To summarise the study, recruitment practices by SMEs are rarely found to involve more than a single interview, with only 13% of firms using further methods (e.g. work-based trial or assessment centres). In addition, only 34% of Polish SMEs have detailed job descriptions to facilitate recruitment, selection and performance management. Further to this, 43% of organisations train employees, but only 28% have an in-house training system. This particular research provides a valuable insight into the prevalence of HRM practices but unfortunately does not provide any specific examples of HRM practices, should they exist, nor does it measure the quality and effectiveness of any formal or informal HR practices.

When looking into SME practice on organisational learning, research by Michna (2009) established positive links with organisational performance. In a study of 211 Polish SMEs, questionnaires were completed to establish links with organisation performance based on 11 dimensions of organisational learning including leader's attitudes, collaboration, team learning and organisational memory. Michna (2009) concluded that while correlations could be made between organisational performance and learning, significant differences were observed between SMEs dependent on their size, age and sector. This particular finding could be seen to develop further on the thought that, contextually, SME organisations can be so diverse that even in relatively small studies, significant differences can be found. A significant relationship between employment growth with dialogue and empowerment of employees is also reported. An explanation can be linked to the high individualist cultural aspect, as we have previously discussed. Conclusions within the study suggest that SME leaders should seek to encourage learning through innovative and experimental methods of work, maintain knowledge and experience and encourage sharing of experience through team collaboration.

Other research by Burke (2011) was undertaken to establish the degree of 'knowledge sharing' within Polish and Hungarian SMEs in comparison with UK SMEs. Knowledge sharing is said to occur through strong social relationships within organisations, and Burke sought to understand what benefits and implications this could bring to SMEs. Burke's results note that barriers are present within Polish SMEs, such as fear and a history of secrecy within organisations, and that these can impact on the success of knowledge sharing. The primary barrier being recorded is the government, and it is associated with specific institutional aspects of the system that facilitate corruption, as we have argued earlier. Burke (2011) also recognises that Eastern European, post-communist countries such as Poland may not necessarily benefit from adopting Western-focused knowledge-sharing practices, but instead research could focus on how successful Polish SMEs practices are in stimulating innovation and organisational success.

In addition to the more conceptual HRM practices of organisational learning and knowledge sharing, Dabic and colleagues (2016) also studied the most frequent and preferred methods of learning and development used in Polish SME organisations. The research was conducted in 100 Polish SMEs. Findings indicated that the most frequently used learning approaches included on-the-job learning and e-learning packages; the least preferred methods involved self-study. When reviewing these findings, Davic et al. (2016) note that the popularity of e-learning packages may well be associated with low-cost implementation. The sector in which SMEs are operating is likely to influence the prevalence of e-learning. For example, it would be more appropriate for a technology or administrative firm to provide training in this manner in comparison with a joinery or a building business.

In relation to talent management practices, there is some research available, but this focuses on Poland's ageing population. As previously mentioned, since 2004, many Polish nationals have immigrated to Western Europe in search of better opportunities. This has inevitably led to a shift in the demand for labour within Poland which has, in turn, lowered unemployment rates in the country. The effect of this on Poland's SME talent pool is further compounded by a high unemployment rate among older workers (Trading Economics, 2018). Zientara (2009) investigated this issue by interviewing Polish SME employers and employees. He found that SME leaders often overlook ageing applicants due to a view that they lack IT skills and are more likely to suffer from ill health. It was also noted that SME employers felt that support should be provided by institutions, such as the State, in offering training opportunities to ageing employees. The older employees interviewed showed high levels of motivation, but they also stressed the importance of flexible working. Zientara (2009) recommended that SMEs show greater awareness of the ability and knowledge base of older employees and that this can help facilitate innovation. This provides a unique but interesting viewpoint on talent management within Polish SMEs when considering the contextual issues they face.

Finally, another important HR practice is performance management. Performance management has been researched by Ates and colleagues (2013). It was found that of the 37 SMEs investigated, 20 acknowledged regular practice for checking individual staff performance. Instead of focusing on individual and employee performance, SMEs were found to focus on traditional organisational tools, such as key performance indicators, short-term goals and financial data when measuring organisational performance. This research offers similar findings with the research by Struzyna et al. (2009), which found that 5% of the SMEs questioned had formal practices for performance management, while 46% had informal practices. Given this informality in performance management practices in SMEs, there is no great scope for linking rewards to performance or for showing appreciation for employee actions and behaviours.

In summary, it appears that Polish SMEs do follow suit with SMEs across the globe in that there is a distinct lack of formalised HRM practices. At the same time, there are clearly some studies arguing in favour of some formal HRM practices in Polish SMEs.

Hungary

Hungary as a transition economy has shown a strong upward trend of GDP growth following the 2012 recession. However, Hungary's income levels have not aligned with this growth and are still significantly lower than more advanced economies (OECD, 2016). Investment as a share of GDP has been rising for the past few years; however, this is mainly by foreign direct investment (FDI) or EU funding (OECD, 2016). This supports the claim that there is a clear lack of domestic business investment by SMEs. Due to economic restructuring, there has been a shift to a more knowledge-based economy, which has seen an expansion in sectors such as IT, telecommunications and business and retail services (OECD, 2016). However, there has been a dramatic decline in employment in industries that are typical of an emerging economy, such as in agriculture, mining and textiles. It is suggested that this is due to economic growth, but the labour market is failing to adapt at the needed rate, hence the creation of a relevant skills shortage (OECD, 2016). A suggested reason for this is the slow reaction from the education system, insufficient outcomes from government schemes and initiatives and the fact that many women in Hungary do not participate in the labour market (OECD, 2016). The lack of women in the labour market could be a significant reason for the skills shortage as the labour market could substantially increase if more was done to encourage women to work.

SMEs in Hungary account for 99.8% of all companies, which emphasises the importance of their success to ensure GDP growth and economic strength (European Commission, 2017). The highest share of SMEs is in wholesale and retail trade, with manufacturing ranked second (European Commission, 2017). The European Commission (2017) supports that only 10.6% of Hungarian SMEs carry out innovation activities. It also suggests that only 10% of Hungarian SMEs are currently selling online, only 4.5% are selling online to other EU member states, and an average of 7.2% of the overall turnover relates to online sales. In addition, the OECD Economic Survey (OECD, 2016) provides a detailed account of the current situation of SMEs, suggesting they are not very competitive, as they suffer from low innovation activity and low productivity, which lead to low competitiveness. Based on this information, it is reasonable to suggest that Hungarian SMEs have a vast potential market if they were to undertake innovative activities and start selling online, further widening their market if they sold to other EU member states.

Domestic business investment by SMEs in Hungary is restricted by the unpredictable, often changing regulatory environment and the high entry barriers in network industries. If reforms were implemented, the economy could see an increase in SME integration into global value chains (OECD, 2016). Additionally, tax policies affect investment because tax systems are frequently changing and this leads to high compliance costs for SMEs (OECD, 2016). Furthermore, the 2009 and 2012 recessions affected financing for domestic SMEs, in comparison with MNCs, who relied on international funding (OECD, 2016). With SMEs relying heavily on domestic credit markets, there is a lot of pressure on banks to provide credit to Hungarian SMEs (OECD, 2016). The government has tried to increase funding for SMEs through some initiatives, such as the 'funding for growth' scheme, which helps to improve the chances of funding for borrowers who are considered a high risk. However, it appears that this initiative has stabilised outstanding loans to SMEs rather than increasing the funding to SMEs (OECD, 2016). Another government initiative is the 'market-based lending' scheme where the central bank accepts responsibility for some of the risk of loans that banks provide to SMEs (OECD, 2016).

Another aspect of Hungary's institutional context is related to its transformation from a socialist regime to a capitalistic market economy. This happened in an abrupt way, which led to many people distrusting the new system and moving in more individualistic directions (Stanojevic, 2014). Additionally, Brewster and Bennett (2010) claim that over 75% of expatriates in Hungary believe that corruption is a significant concern when conducting business there. Based on this, people set up their own businesses to avoid betrayal and maintain control during a post-communist context where fear is high.

As competitiveness from international MNCs increases, domestic SMEs have been exposed due to their weak competitive nature (Richbell et al., 2010). The previous Socialist regime in Hungary is to blame because certain practices are still embedded today. An example of such past practices limiting SMEs today is the ban on entrepreneurship, which discourages private business initiatives (Richbell et al., 2010). Furthermore, Richbell et al. (2010) suggest that low competitiveness is linked to poorly developed cultural aspects. Entrepreneurs believe that the high tax and social security burden are to blame, including the unpredictability of government policy. However, the government blame SMEs and their lack of three key elements: innovation strategies, entrepreneurial and managerial skills and well-developed networks (Richbell et al., 2010). Moreover, the importance of networks for the emerging SME market in Hungary has been identified for gaining valuable knowledge to aid expansion nationally and internationally (Richbell et al., 2010). However, reflecting on the fact that only 4.5% of SMEs in Hungary sell online to other EU member states, this opportunity is evidently not being utilised. In a similar vein, Jormanainen and Koveshnikov (2012) support that various networks and entrepreneurial activity are important for successful SME expansion into international markets. However, since Hungarian SMEs are suffering from low productivity and innovation, as previously discussed, it is likely that they will struggle to expand both nationally and internationally (OECD, 2016).

The application of HR practices in Hungarian SMEs depends on various factors. For example, the fact that 94.3% of all companies in Hungary are micro-sized (European Commission, 2017) means that the majority of companies in Hungary have less than ten employees. It is reasonable to conclude from this that the vast majority of SMEs in Hungary do not have a formal HR policy. Furthermore, Kiss and Poor (2006) suggest that SMEs are unable to pay HRM consultancies for accessing HR expertise and knowledge. The informality of HRM in SMEs in Hungary and their inability to access HR expertise externally leaves them without HRM knowledge.

Richbell et al. (2010) conducted a survey of 678 SMEs in Hungary, and the findings suggest that working relationships in Hungarian SMEs are closer to the 'small is beautiful' perspective. An interesting finding of this survey was the minimal number of SMEs who identified skills shortages as being an issue, as this is often highlighted as a problem in other economies (European Commission, 2017). Furthermore, Richbell et al. (2010) support the view that poorly developed and limited government training initiatives fail to provide the required support to enhance and expand SMEs. As previously highlighted, with the majority of SMEs being without formal HR policies, they rely heavily on government initiatives to support them with training needs. A study conducted by Mako (2005) found that only a third of SMEs in Hungary offer training for staff with only a slight increase for medium-sized firms. This is significantly lower and also less formal and structured than large firms in Hungary (Mako, 2005).

Regarding employee resourcing, Karoliny et al. (2009) conducted a study focusing on Hungarian characteristics of HRM in 97 companies. The study examined recruitment and selection and found that for management positions in Hungary, the use of headhunters is a popular method, while job advertisements are placed only 9% of the time. In addition, this study found that 'word of mouth' was ranked in the top three recruitment methods. Electronic recruitment was found to be an infrequently used method, which is an unsurprising result based on the minimal number of companies in Hungary who sell online and the low innovation activity (OECD, 2016). Recruitment and selection problems are identified by Kiss and Poor (2006) as being linked to the lack of accessibility to skilled HRM consultants. However, as previously mentioned, Richbell et al. (2010) found that Hungarian SMEs do not perceive there to be a significant problem with skills gaps. This means that SMEs do not feel that they need external support or simply cannot afford to access this support.

In terms of working arrangements, overtime is one of the most frequently used working arrangements, especially when a company is in the expansion stages, including taking on more people (Karoliny et al., 2009). In a similar vein, job sharing was found to be a rarely adopted method, but a very useful one, in getting women to contribute to the labour market, enabling them to have an achievable work-life balance (Karoliny et al., 2009). It is suggested by the OECD (2016) that part-time and flexible working patterns are rarely used in Hungary. A study by Toth (2005) found that although the EU is encouraging policies regarding flexible working, there is still a lot of development needed on other policies in Hungarian companies before they can develop these policies to an EU standard. However, as previously discussed, SMEs feel the burden of social security via frequently changing tax policies that are costly to SMEs (OECD, 2016). Drahokoupil et al. (2015) claim that flexible working arrangement resistance from Hungarian companies is becoming a serious issue and is now causing conflict between trade unions and these companies.

As far as performance appraisals is concerned, the study by Karoliny et al. (2009) reported a surprising finding on the wide use of performance appraisals, which also puts Hungarian practice in line with developed European countries. Furthermore, with regard to training and development, the study found internal training as the most common method of training, likely due to its inexpensive nature and the lack of external support for SMEs. Moreover, employee relations and communication, specifically to brief staff on business performance, was quite low (Karoliny et al., 2009). Hungary was identified to have a significant increase in the use of electronic communication, but the main preference is still communication via managers. This could be due to the high proportion of companies in Hungary having less than ten employees (European Commission, 2017), allowing face-to-face communication to be more appropriate and effective.

In summary, HR practices in Hungarian SMEs have gone through significant changes. The speed of changes in HRM practices has been one of the fastest in the CEE region (Karoliny et al., 2009). However, low innovation activity, lack of entrepreneurial and managerial skills and poor networks have been identified as leading limiting factors for SMEs.

The Czech Republic

The Czech Republic's economy depends on foreign demand. It is mainly broken down into trade, transport manufacturing and construction. However, agriculture is slowly developing, which will hopefully contribute to unemployment figures decreasing. The Czech economy has been facilitated during the last decade with restructuring and liberalisation and does show signs of laissez-faire elements as in a free market. Farnham (2015) reports economic decisions about allocation of resources and production of services are generated by economic exchanges among producers, consumers and owners of the factors of production. The Czech economy has a neo-liberalistic approach, looking at protecting its economic growth and political freedom. Open-market policies sustaining global trade and investment flows enable the economy to capitalise on regulatory efficiencies achieved through earlier reforms, which are mainly based on legitimate restrictions and social expectations (Roth and O'Donnell, 1996). Enterprises in the Czech Republic were greatly affected by the 2008 economic crisis, when employment decreased by 28%. There was also a high number of companies that became bankrupt because of that reason (OECD, 2016). According to the OECD (2016), reforms should be encouraged to allow successful firms to expand, if desired, and for unproductive firms to endeavour to exist more easily.

The Czech economy consists of mainly microenterprises (Czech Statistical Office, 2018) with 92.5% of enterprises employing less than ten employees. SMEs represent 7.3% of all companies and large enterprises represent 0.2%. Most SMEs are state-owned or privatised, especially in the manufacturing and production industry. In Prague, it has been estimated that approximately 54,000 people are business owners, of which, according to Koudelkova (2014), 70% decided to start their business due to an opportunity that occurred in the market or due to unemployment. Survival continues to be a challenge to many SMEs' existence in the Czech economy as they tend to draw heavily on existing social, ethnic and cultural ties (Cooke et al., 2011) that cut across national boundaries and are more likely to draw upon specialised local knowledge as a means of competitive advantage. Showing flexibility and increasing pay to gain skilled staff and being able to adjust to supply and demand should assist in this challenge. In addition, innovation is crucial to the growth of Czech SMEs. In this respect, Koudelkova (2014) argues that it should become a top priority for government strategies and policies in order to stimulate economic growth and business development.

The Czech government has put in place programmes to encourage higher business spending by encouraging firms to mobilise their own resources. However, this is where diligence is needed as some internal resource methods could be exploited here: for example, using employees already in the company to fill posts even if not trained up to the position. A few years ago, the government approved the amendments to the Labour Code prepared by the Ministry of Labour and Social Affairs. This is expected to lead to changes in rules when concluding agreements on work activity (e.g. giving employees the right to statutory holidays), regulations on homeworking and teleworking (e.g. working hours, same rights), provisions relating to an easier return to work after parental leave, etc. This last reform attempted to enhance HR practices within Czech firms.

Nevertheless, as Horvathova (2011) argues, many companies in the Czech Republic avoid thinking strategically about the future, instead following a reactive approach. This means that they also avoid thinking strategically in terms of their human resources. Therefore, it comes as no surprise that the situation is the same within SMEs. Czech SMEs avoid introducing formal HRM practices as they do not possess the resources required to implement such practices. Some owners do not consider that such practices can contribute to the company's competitive advantage and consider them as an unnecessary cost. Employee performance is underestimated as only a minority of Czech SMEs use any form of appraisal/development system, showing a low commitment strategy to a crucial aspect of the organisation. With this lack of performance management strategy, the sharing and transferring of knowledge is not encouraged by employers. This seems to influence HR development practices such as talent management. As it has been reported by Horvathova (2011), one of the main reasons that talent management is not implemented in SMEs in the Czech Republic is that it is not fully understood by business owners, and when some form of development is carried out, it is usually only targeted at key individuals and is not widely available.

In summary, HRM in Czech SMEs seems to be critically underdeveloped, mainly due to the small size of these firms. Business survival continues to be a challenge for SMEs, and this increases the need for SMEs to be flexible and adaptable.

Slovenia

Slovenia used to be part of Yugoslavia but is now classified as a post-communist and independent country. Slovenia joined Europe in 2004 and was the first new member to adopt the Euro currency in 2007. As a country, it is characterised by a highly educated workforce, which is a likely consequence of having a solid educational system in the country. Its education system ranks as the twelfth best in the world and fourth best in the EU. The majority of the population is Slovene, with lower levels of immigrants from other European countries. Its economy is considered small, open and focused on exportation, with low levels of FDI. The country is largely dependent on its own economy rather than on European funding. Slovenia's main economic field is services, followed by industry and construction (Lahovnik and Malenkovic, 2011). Prior to 2008, Slovenia was considered as one of the best economic performers in Europe, but the global financial crisis brought many challenges to its economy.

Slovenia's political situation can be described as having an established democratic political regime, that of political pluralism. The government in Slovenia has preserved a well-developed social welfare system and worked towards preventing social exclusion, mainly by having influence over taxation and employment, as well as by providing grants and by manipulating policies on housing, family, healthcare and education. To understand Slovenia's culture and particularly how it might affect workplace attitudes, we can consider Hofstede's analysis (Hofstede Insights, 2018). Hofstede has found that Slovenia is characterised by what he calls a high power distance, meaning that people have a general acceptance of authority. Their culture is also identified as having low individualism, which suggests a collectivistic society where teamwork and relationships are important. In a working environment, this characterisation would suggest that recruitment and promotions will rely, to some degree, on an employee's in-group and companies would focus on the management of groups rather than individuals. Hofstede categorises Slovenia as a feminist society, which suggests that Slovenians would rather work to live than live to work. It also suggests that managers in Slovenian businesses strive for consensus between themselves and employees, and that employees value free time and flexible working highly. They would typically place importance on employee well-being and would work towards resolving conflicts with compromise and negotiation. Slovenia scores high on uncertainty avoidance, meaning that people will have an emotional need for rules and regulations. This element suggests that Slovenes will have an inner urge to work hard and will place high importance on feeling secure.

When considering the impact on Slovenian SMEs, it is also important to consider institutional perspectives. Hardy (2002) talks about 'local isomorphism', that is, the conditioning effects of the local environment, which is more likely to impact HR practices because of the constraints of the country's regulations and practices. For example, issues such as wages, hours of work, job contracts and redundancy procedures are often subject to local institutional influence. As briefly discussed before, the Slovenian government provides funding for SMEs to stimulate the economy. To limit the negative effects of the 2008 crisis in employment, the government introduced measures targeted at employment issues in the labour market. This included providing partial funding to allow employees being temporarily laid off and subsidising a shorter working week (Kresal, 2010). Kresal (2010) highlights that economic policies which focus on labour markets must find a fair balance between employer and employee interests in regulations covering dismissal in an economic crisis, including collective dismissals. He also suggests that the government needs to strengthen the importance of training and development as well as strengthen the labour market policy further overall.

However, it must be highlighted that corruption has been seen as a risk for businesses operating in Slovenia, as there is an overlap between organisations and politics, which has a particularly damaging effect on public procurement (GAM Integrity, 2015). Although it has been found that there is low risk associated with the police, public services and tax, there is a higher amount of risk identified with the judicial system as bribes do occur (Schwab and Sala-i-Martin, 2016). GAM Integrity (2015) reported that one in ten firms find the courts to be a major block for doing business in Slovenia, which puts added pressure on SMEs. Further to these local controls, SMEs are subject to regulation at regional and international levels. As previously discussed, it is worth considering the impact of the EU as an institution itself. In 2013, exports represented 70% of Slovenian GDP, and of these, 68.98% were to other EU countries (OECD, 2013). Therefore, the Slovenian economy is highly dependent on the EU economy. When in economic crisis, Slovenian SMEs will need to consider their international position. When Slovenia joined the EU in 2004, it became subject to employment legislation dictated by the EU. This means that policies such as the working time directive and other employment protection could limit SMEs when there is a need to make savings on labour costs.

The institutions explained earlier have a profound impact on HRM practices adopted in various companies, including SMEs. SMEs have not been greatly studied in relation to HRM in Slovenia (Šušnjar et al., 2016). Suutari (1998) supports that this is due to the rapid economic, social and political changes in central Europe where Slovenia is situated, leading to a lack of knowledge practices and work relationships in post-communist countries. As the dust settles for Slovenia and its GDP starts to rise again, we will hopefully see this change and begin to understand its position more.

To better understand how Slovenian SMEs adopt HR practices, we can start by looking at Slovenia's use of HRM as a whole. Brewster et al. (2004) found that Slovenia had a long tradition of professionalism in HR, which could be connected to their strong educational system. In fact, HRM courses for managers started as early as the 1950s and could be studied at a master's level, similarly to the UK. However as pointed out by Brewster and colleagues, it appears that, in practice, they tend to use more traditional personnel management than modern HRM.

To consider its history, research by Svetlik et al. (2010) explains how prior to becoming independent, countries that were part of Yugoslavia, such as Slovenia, were tightly controlled by the state. Management was not assumed as a reputable profession and promotion was not linked to performance (Pearce, 1991). It was general practice that the personnel director, as the position was called then, would have to be politically accepted, and therefore, the idea of modern politically neutral leadership did not exist. When Slovenia became independent in 1991, this gave way to a more professional approach, although it is likely that part of this history will still be evident in organisations today, and especially in SMEs, which are more likely to use traditional personnel approaches.

Svetlik et al. (2010) highlight that foreign businesses did a lot for bringing modern HR practices to Slovenia and that they indirectly contributed to the spread of modern HR practices to their neighbouring countries, which suggests that they have better understanding of how HR can help in challenging times. Šušnjar et al. (2016) identified that Slovenian SMEs use mostly informal HR approaches for recruitment, performance, training and remuneration. However, they were also able to suggest that Slovenian SMEs have shown higher levels of strategic HRM due to the fact that they are more likely to have an HR department, where more formal methods would typically be used.

Eurofound (2013) highlighted that restructuring in SMEs is now a permanent feature of the Slovenian economy since the financial crisis. Therefore, there is pressure on HR to ensure that this process is implemented correctly as well as to ensure that motivation does not affect the performance of employees who remain in work after the implementation of redundancies. Moreover, Šušnjar et al. (2016) found that among those SMEs in Slovenia that did run talent management programmes, there was actually little to no managerial understanding of how the right talent can be found, suggesting that SMEs lack the knowledge needed.

Furthermore, Eurofound (2013) looked into industrial relations in Slovenia during the economic crisis and found that it generally did not undergo any major changes in composition. This study found that there were breaches of collective agreements from employers, particularly around pay. The report did find an increase in hasty and unilateral government interventions into public sector working conditions. However, a recent Eurofound (2016) report found that Slovenian SMEs rarely have powerful trade unions which they can use to negotiate good conditions for redundant employees.

In summary, Slovenian SMEs seem to be keen to apply various HRM practices based on the logic of their expansion and further development. In other words, although there are some critical institutional factors affecting HRM, SMEs tend to follow modern management practices especially when they try to expand their businesses at international levels through collaborations with foreign companies.

Bulgaria

Bulgaria is a former socialist country which joined the EU in 2007. It has a relatively unstable political environment, and this is affecting economic success and investment levels (European Commission, 2017; Lipset and Lenz, 2000; Sandholtz and Tagepera, 2005). Bulgarian SMEs represent 99.8% of all enterprises, and this shows their importance within the Bulgarian economy (European Commission, 2017). The fact that the majority of SMEs are small enterprises has implications for management and HRM practices.

The declining role of the state in Bulgaria allowed a market-oriented system of employment, supported by the reforming of formal and informal institutions (Williams and Vorley, 2015). Tanova and Nadiri (2010) claim that Bulgaria is a high-context culture, affecting employee voice and communication in SMEs. Bulgarian culture is centred on high power distance, collectivism and extreme levels of high uncertainty, similar to Slovenia, showing adaption to uncertain business conditions (Brewster et al., 2016; Hofstede, 2016; Minkov and Hofstede, 2014). The literature argues that Bulgarian culture was the reason behind corruption, caused by certain behaviours, arising from social pressures and viewed as the norm in communist times (Lipset and Lenz, 2000; Miller et al., 2001; Sandholtz and Tagepera, 2005).

The institutional context of Bulgaria also has a critical influence over its business system. Garcia-Cabrera et al. (2016) mention EU regulative institutions influence SMEs through coercive pressures. Preventing unfair practices and employment law is essential, but the assumption in Bulgaria is that legislation is low priority or non-existent. However, legislation is present, but weak enforcement from institutions prevents implementation, allowing informal practices (e.g. corruption) to take precedent (Meyer and Peng, 2015). Moreover, the Bulgarian government is too weak to enforce law, leading to unregulated actors within the market-oriented system who are capable of exploiting SME environments.

Recently, corruption has been studied in relation to its link with institutional networks within Bulgaria. Brewster and Bennett (2010) studied the business culture and found corruption present in the way management relationships and business transactions operate, similar to Eastern and Arab countries. Bulgarian corruption is higher than other CEE countries, shown by ranking 69 on the public sector corruption chart, comparable to Jamaica and behind Serbia. The main reason for Bulgarian corruption is the weak institutions, which according to the EU lead to reduced investments and prevents fast scale development

(European Commission, 2017). However, many claim that EU membership will reduce corruption levels (Lipset and Lenz, 2000; Sandholtz and Tagepera). Emerson (2006) challenges this, arguing that Bulgarian institutions encourage corruption and no amount of policies or EU interference can change this, since corruption is part of Bulgaria's adaption to democracy. Corruption is considered as the path of survival among Bulgarian SMEs (Lipset and Lenz, 2000; Sandholtz and Tagepera, 2005; William and Vorley, 2015).

Hyder and Abraha (2008) state that institutional and cultural factors overlap, affecting performance and HRM practices implemented in SMEs. Bulgarian SMEs deal with HRM practices in a divergent way, influenced by culture and pressures from institutions and competitors. HRM practices in Bulgarian SMEs are affected by cultural variables. The organisational and societal cultural levels influence managers' behaviour and relationships (Aycan et al., 2000; Vadi and Vereshagin, 2006). A high power distance culture influences the management style, which impacts on communication and HRM practices (Tung and Aycan, 2008). SMEs often operate as a family unit with close relationships, which is encouraged by Bulgaria's collective culture. Pucetaite et al. (2006) and Vadi and Vereshagin (2006) state that performance management and training should always consider the group, which influences the implementation of HRM practices. Vadi and Vereshagin (2006) discuss how a collectivistic culture impacts on HRM practices, as trust is critical to the employment relationship and Bulgarian employees are still fearful of management after the communist regime.

Institutions influence SMEs and the behaviour of employees and management steer towards certain HRM practices (Psychogios and Wood, 2010). Social values have led to normative pressures on SMEs, with corruption seen as acceptable practice and institutions developed to reduce risk, showing adaptation to the high uncertainty avoidance culture (Garcia-Cabrera et al., 2016).

In Bulgarian SMEs, formal HRM functions are rare, and implementation of in-house resources are not cost-effective and have no tangible benefit. Instead, SMEs customise their HRM practices, as the majority employ less than ten employees (Kazlauskaite et al., 2013; Wilkinson, 1999). Indeed, Šušnjar et al. (2016) researched Bulgarian SMEs and found that only 34.9% had a formal HRM function, backing up Wilkinson's (1999) argument that HRM functions are rare in small businesses. Instead of HRM functions, it is the owners or line managers in SMEs who are responsible for HRM. For example, owners or line managers make decisions about pay and rewards. Many Bulgarian SMEs are family-owned and flexible with informal HRM practices, allowing an emergent approach towards decision-making and reduced bureaucracy (Dundon and Wilkinson, 2009; Psychogios and Wood, 2010; Šušnjar et al., 2016). Behrends (2007) argues that HRM, both formal and informal, can be implemented in SMEs in Bulgaria. SMEs can have formal HRM practices; however, if the resources and time to implement is not considered, they could become informal practices (Psychogios et al., 2016).

Dundon and Wilkinson (2009) and Kinnie et al. (1999) mention that SME size impacts on formal HRM practices. The majority of Bulgarian SMEs employ less than ten people, as we have previously discussed; therefore, informal HR practices are most common. However, variation in Bulgarian HRM practices is dependent on SME sector and size. SMEs based in manufacturing employ lower skilled workers compared with the IT industry, which stereotypically employs higher-skilled workers. Sector influences the amount of formal HRM. The increased competition for highly skilled talent encourages the adoption of formal HRM practices; however, lower skilled workers can be exploited through informal practices (Bacon and Hoque, 2005).

In summary, current research shows that Bulgarian SMEs have become influential within the business environment and that HRM practices have adapted to the cultural and institutional aspects of the post-communist context in Bulgaria. Divergent HRM practices have resulted in both informal and formal HRM practices being present within SMEs. Bulgarian SMEs face unique issues, which the EU's Small Business Act (SBA) is trying to solve. However, the SBA is a set of universal aims not aligned to Bulgaria's business context and has made little difference to SME performance and development. Both cultural and institutional pressures are evident within Bulgarian SMEs. The high-powered cultural context and weak enforcement is demonstrated in the autocratic management styles, along with the collective approaches to reward and training. In emergent economies, institutions are an essential part of the environment, and weak enforcement influences HRM practices in Bulgaria. Institutional pressures from the EU have created an isomorphic type of HRM practice, and weak institutions have allowed informal practices (e.g. corruption) to influence HRM. As a result, corruption is engrained within society. The EU maintains that business attitudes and corruption should be removed from SMEs; however, they fail to account that corruption 'works' for Bulgarian SMEs.

Summary

Chapter 6 explored HRM in SMEs in transition economies of Central and Eastern Europe. The past autarchic environment of state control in these countries means that entrepreneurial development has been slow and foreign investments limited. MNCs operating in the market can influence management thinking and practices in local SMEs. However, the owner usually manages SMEs in these countries, and for this reason, they develop their own informal way of working based on resources and expertise. Unregulated informal economic activities are a common feature in this region. Our analysis suggests that smaller businesses in transition economies do not have formalised HRM functions, but we note the additional influence of the specific business context in which the SMEs operate. This chapter also supports the argument that there are three antecedents of the formalisation of HRM practice in SMEs operating in a post-communist context, namely, the degree of internationalisation of SMEs, the sector of SMEs and the size of SMEs. In other words, SMEs in transition economies tend to adopt formal HR practices either because they are growing in size or because they are expanding internationally. Finally, SMEs in the manufacturing sector seem to be keener to apply a range of HRM practices, which can be explained by their often larger size and range of international collaborations. The next chapter explores the challenges faced by SMEs in European economic crisis contexts.

References

Ates, A., Garengo, P., Cocca, P. and Bititci, U. (2013). The development of SME managerial practice for effective performance management. *Journal of Small Business and Enterprise Development*, 20(1): pp. 28–54.

Aycan, Z., Kanungo, R. M., Mendonca, M., Yu, K., Stahl, G. and Kurshid, A. (2000). Impact of culture on human resource management practices: A 10-country comparison. *Applied Psychology*, 49(1): pp. 192–221.

Bacon, N. and Hoque, K. (2005). HRM in the SME sector: Valuable employees and coercive networks. *International Journal of Human Resources Management*, 16: pp. 1976–1999.

Batt, R., Holman, D. and Holtgrewe, U. (2009). The globalization of service work: Comparative institutional perspectives on call centers. *Industrial and Labor Relations Review*, 62(4): pp. 453–488.

Behrends, T. (2007). Recruitment practices in small and medium size enterprises: An empirical study among knowledge-intensive professional service firms. *Management Review*, 18(1): pp. 55–74.

Bluhm, K. and Schmidt, R. (2008). *Change in SMEs: Towards a New European Capitalism?* Basingstoke: Palgrave Macmillan.

Bogicevic Milikic, B., Janicijevic, N. and Petkovic, M. (2008). HRM in transition economies: The case of Serbia. *South East European Journal of Economics and Business*, 3(2): pp. 75–88.

Brewster, C. and Bennett, V. C. (2010). Perceptions of business cultures in Eastern Europe and their implications for international HRM. *The International Journal of Human Resource Management*, 21(14): pp. 2568–2588.

Brewster, C., Houldsworth, E., Sparrow, P. and Vernon, G. (2016). *International Human Resource Management*. (4th edition). London: CIPD.

Brewster, C., Mayrhofer, W. and Morley, M. (2004). *Human Resource Management in Europe: Evidence of Convergence?* Oxford: Elsevier Butterworth-Heinemann.

Brewster, C., Morley, M. and Buciuniene, I. (2010). The reality of human resource management in Central and Eastern Europe. *Baltic Journal of Management*, 5(2): pp. 145–155.

Burke, M. E. (2011). Knowledge sharing in emerging economies. *Library Review*, 60(1): pp. 5–14.

Cooke, F. L., Wood, G., Psychogios, A. G. and Szamosi, L. T. (2011). HRM in emergent market economies: Evidence and implications from Europe. *Human Resource Management Journal*, 21(4): pp. 368–378.

Czech Statistical Office (2018). *Statistics*. [online]. Available at: www.czso.cz/csu/czso/statistics. [Accessed 1 September 2018].

Dabic, M., Vlajcic, D. and Novak, I. (2016). Entrepreneurial management education needs in the Republic of Croatia, Poland and the United Kingdom. *International Journal of Educational Management*, 30(6): pp. 738–755.

Drahokoupil, J., Myant, M. and Domonkos, S. (2015). The politics of flexibility: Employment practices in automotive multinationals in Central and Eastern Europe. *European Journal of Industrial Relations*, 21(3): pp. 223–240.

Dundon, T. and Wilkinson, A. (2009). HRM in small and medium sized enterprises (SMEs). In D. G. Collings, T. W. Geoffrey, eds., *Human Resource Management. A Critical Approach*. London: Routledge, pp. 130–147.

Emerson, S. M. (2006). Corruption in Bulgaria. *Public Integrity*, 8(1): pp. 65–76.

Eurofound (2013). *Slovenia: Impact of the crisis on industrial relations*. [online]. Available at www.eurofound.europa.eu/observatories/eurwork/comparative-information/national-contributions/slovenia/slovenia-impact-of-the-crisis-on-industrial-relations. [Accessed 1 September 2018].

Eurofound (2016). *Start-up Support for Young People in the EU: From Implementation to Evaluation*. Luxembourg: Publications Office of the European Union.

European Commission (2017). *2016 SBA fact sheet: Hungary*. [online]. Available at: https://ec.europa.eu/docsroom/documents/22382/attachments/16/translations/en/renditions/pdf. [Accessed 1 September 2018].

Farnham, D. (2015). *Human Resource Management in Context: Insights, Strategy and Solutions*. (4th edition). London: Chartered Institute of Personnel and Development.

Feige, E. L. (1991). Perestroika and ruble convertibility. *Cato Journal*, 10(3): pp. 631–653.

Feige, E. L. (2017). The transition to a market economy in Russia: Property rights, mass privatisation and stabilisation. In G. S. Alexander and G. Skapska, eds., *A Fourth Way? Privatisation, Property and the Emergence of New Market Economics*. Oxon: Routledge, pp. 81–102.

GAM Integrity (2015). *Slovenia corruption report*. [online]. Available at: www.business-anti-corruption.com/country-profiles/slovenia. [Accessed 1 September 2018].

Garcia-Cabrera, A. M., Casademunt, A. M. L. and Cuellar-Molina, D. (2016). Institutions and human resource practices in European countries. *The International Journal of Human Resource Management*, published online, DOI: 10.1080/09585192.2016.1239119.

Hall, P. A. and Soskice, D. (eds.) (2001). *Varieties of Capitalism: The Institutional Foundations of Comparative Advantage*. Oxford: Oxford University Press.

Hardy, J. A. (2002). *An institutionalist analysis of foreign investment in Poland: Wroclaw's second great transformation*. Doctoral dissertation, Durham University.

Hofstede, G. (2011). *Dimensionalizing cultures: The Hofstede model in context*. [online]. Available at: https://scholarworks.gvsu.edu/orpc/vol2/iss1/8/?&sa=

U&ei=9owuVLrgCIfXaqzngIgJ&ved=0CEsQFjAJ&usg=AFQjCNFBrStE0 AJaAVPLrpU8s-lDqibYvw. [Accessed 1 September 2018].

Hofstede Insights (2018). *Slovenia*. [online]. Available at: www.hofstede-insights. com/country/slovenia/. [Accessed 1 September 2018].

Horvathova, P. (2011). *Talent management*. Prague: Wolters Kluwer.

Hyder, A. S. and Abraha, D. (2008). Institutional factors and strategic alliances in Eastern and Central Europe. *Baltic Journal of Management*, 3(3): pp. 289–308.

Jormanainen, I. and Koveshnikov, P. C.A. (2012). International activities of emerging market firms. *Management International Review*, 52(5): pp. 691–725.

Karoliny, Z., Farkas, F. and Poor, J. (2009). In focus: Hungarian and Central Eastern European characteristics of human resource management - an international comparative survey. *Journal of East European Management Studies*, 14(1): pp. 9–47.

Kazlauskaite, R., Buciuniene, I., Poor, J., Karoliny, Z., Alas, R., Kohont, A. and Szlavicz, A. (2013). Human resource management in the Central and Eastern European Region. In E. Parry, E. Stavrou and M. Lazarova, eds., *Global Trends in Human Resource Management*. Basingstoke: Palgrave Macmillan, pp. 103–121.

Kinnie, N., Purcell, J., Hutchinson, S., Terry, M., Collinson, M. and Scarborough, H. (1999). Employment relations in SMEs: Market driven or customer shaped? *Employee Relations*. 21(3): pp. 218–236.

Kiss, K. and Poor, J. (2006). Management and HR characteristics of SMEs in Hungarian regions in the framework of the Life-Cycle model. *Munkangyi Szemle*, 50(9): pp. 14–19.

Koudelkova, P. (2014). Innovation in small and medium enterprises in the Czech Republic. *Central European Business Review*, 3(3): pp. 31–37.

Kresal, B. (2010). *Restructuring in Slovenia*. Draft paper for the Anticipating and Managing Restructuring in Enterprises National Seminars (A.R.E. NA.S), International Training Centre–ILO.

Kuruvilla, S. and Ranganathan, A. (2009). Economic development strategies and macro- and micro-level human resource policies: The case of India's outsourcing industry. *Industrial and Labor Relations Review*, 62(1): pp. 39–72.

Lahovnik, M. and Malenkovic, V. (2011). Corporate acquisition strategies and economic performance: A case of Slovenia, Proceedings of Rijeka Faculty of Economics. *Journal of Economics and Business*, 29(1): pp. 33–50.

Lane, D. (2007). Post-state socialism: A diversity of capitalisms? In D. Lane and M. Myant, eds., *Varieties of Capitalism in Post-Communist Countries*. London: Palgrave, pp. 13–39.

Lipset, S. M. and Lenz, G. S. (2000). Corruption, culture and markets. In L. E. Harrison and S. P. Huntington, eds., *Culture Matters: How Values Shape Human Progress*. New York: Basic Books, pp. 112–124.

Maczynski, J., Zamorska, J. and Lobodzinski, A. (2010). Differences on organisational practices between Polish managers studied in 1996/1997 and 2008/2009. *Journal of Intercultural Management*, 2(1): pp. 69–77.

Mako, C. (2005). Training and competence development in the SME Sector: The Hungarian case. *Journal for East European Management Studies*, 10(2): pp. 156–185.

Meyer, K. E. and Peng, M. W. (2015). Theoretical foundations of emerging economy business research. *Journal of International Business Studies*, 47(1): pp. 3–22.

Michailova, S., Heraty, N. and Morley, M. (2009). Studying human resource management in the international context: The case of Central and Eastern Europe. In M. Morley, N. Heraty and S. Michailova, eds., *Managing Human Resources in Central and Eastern Europe*. London and New York: Routledge, pp. 1–24.

Michna, A. (2009). The relationship between organisational learning and SME performance in Poland. *Journal of European Industrial Training*, 33(4): 356–370.

Miller, W. L., Grodeland, A. B. and Koshechkina, T. Y. (2001). *A Culture of Corruption: Coping with Government in Post-Communist Europe*. New York: Central European University Press.

Minkov, M. and Hofstede, G. (2014). A replication of Hofstede's uncertainty avoidance dimension across nationally representative samples from Europe. *International Journal of Cross Cultural Management*, 14(2): pp. 161–171.

Morley, M., Heraty, N. and Michailova, S. (2009). *Managing Human Resources in Central and Eastern Europe*. London and New York: Routledge, pp. 1–24.

OECD (2013). *OECD economic surveys: Slovenia 2013*. [online]. Available at: http://dx.doi.org/10.1787/eco.surveys-sun-2013-en. [Accessed 1 September 2018].

OECD (2016). *Economic survey of Hungary 2016*. [online]. Available at: www.oecd.org/hungary/economic-survey-hungary.htm. [Accessed 1 September 2018].

OECD (2018). *International migration database*. [online]. Available at: https://stats.oecd.org/Index.aspx?DataSetCode=MIG. [Accessed 1 September 2018].

Pagano, M. and Volpin, P. F. (2005). The political economy of corporate governance. *American Economic Review*, 95(4): pp. 1005–1030.

Pearce, J. L. (1991). From socialism to capitalism; the effects of Hungarian human resources practices. *Academy of Management Perspectives*, 5(4): pp. 75–88.

Psychogios, A. G., Brewster, C., Missopoulos, F., Kohont, A., Vatchkova, E. and Slavic, A. (2014). Industrial relations in South East Europe: Disaggregating the contexts. *The International Journal of Human Resource Management*, 25(11): pp. 1592–1612.

Psychogios, A. G., Szamosi, T. L., Prouska, R. and Brewster, C. (2016). A three-fold framework for understanding HRM practices in South-Eastern European SMEs. *Employee Relations*, 38(3): pp. 310–331.

Psychogios, A. G. and Wood, G. (2010). Human resource management in comparative perspective: Alternative institutionalist perspectives and empirical realities. *The International Journal of Human Resource Management*, 21(4): pp. 2614–2630.

Pucetaite, R., Lamsa, A. M. and Novelskaite, A. (2006). Building organisational trust in a low-trust societal context. *Baltic Journal of Management*, 5(2): pp. 197–217.

Richbell, S., Szerb, L. and Vitai, Z. (2010). HRM in the Hungarian SME sector. *Employee Relations*, 32(3): pp. 262–280.

Roberts, K. (2001). The new east European model of education, training and youth employment. *Journal of Education and Work*, 14(3): pp. 315–328.

Roe, M. (2003). *Political Determinants of Corporate Governance*. Oxford University Press.

Roth, K. and O'Donnell, S. (1996). Foreign subsidiary compensation strategy: An agency theory perspective. *Academy of Management Journal*, 39: pp. 678–703.

Sandholtz, W. and Taagepera, R. (2005). Corruption, culture and communism. *International Review of Sociology*, 15(1): pp. 109–131.

Schwab, K. and Sala-i-Martin, X. (2016). The global competitiveness report 2015–2016, Geneva. *The World Economic Forum*, 403: pp. 1–92.

Schwartz, G. and McCann, L. (2007). Overlapping effects: Path dependence and path generation in management and organisation in Russia. *Human Relations*, 60(10): pp. 1525–1549.

Stanojevic, M. (2014). Conditions for a neoliberal turn: The cases of Hungary and Slovenia. *European Journal of Industrial Relations*, 20(2): pp. 97–112.

Stark, D. and Bruszt, L. (1998). *Postsocialist Pathways. Transforming Politics and Property in East Central Europe*. Cambridge: Cambridge University Press.

Struzyna, J., Ingram, T. and Kraus, S. (2009). Human resource management in small enterprises from Poland. In M. Fink and S. Kraus, eds., *The Management of Small and Medium Enterprises*. New York: Routledge, pp. 125–141.

Šušnjar, G. Š., Slavić, A., Berber, N. and Leković, B. (2016). The role of human resource management in small and medium sized companies in Central-Eastern Europe. In J. Ateljević and J. Trivić, eds., *Economic Development and Entrepreneurship in Transition Economies*. Springer, [eBook], pp. 205–229.

Sutch, H., Wojciechowicz, J. and Dybula, M. (1999). *Corruption in Poland: Review of priority areas and proposals for action (English)*. World Bank. [online]. Available at: http://documents.worldbank.org/curated/en/790651468092376183/Corruption-in-Poland-review-of-priority-areas-and-proposals-for-action. [Accessed 1 September 2018].

Suutari, V. (1998). Leadership behaviour in Eastern Europe: Finnish expatriates' experiences in Russia and Estonia. *The International Journal of Human Resource Management*, 9(2): pp. 235–258.

Svetlik, I., Barisic, A. F., Kohont, A., Petkovic, M., Miric, A. A., Slavic, A., Vaupot, Z. and Poor, J. (2010). Human resource management in the countries of the former Yugoslavia. *Review of International Comparative Management*, 11(5): pp. 807–833.

Szamosi, L. T., Wilkinson, A., Wood, G. and Psychogios, A. G. (2010). Developments in HRM in south-eastern Europe. *The International Journal of Human Resource Management*, 21(14): pp. 2521–2528.

Tanova, C. and Nadiri, H. (2010). The role of cultural context in direct communication. *Baltic Journal of Management*, 5(2): pp. 185–196.

Toth, H. (2005) Gendered dilemmas of the work–life balance in Hungary. *Women in Management Review*, 20 (5): pp. 361–375.

Trading Economics (2018). *Poland unemployment rate 1990–2018*. [online]. Available at: https://tradingeconomics.com/poland/unemployment-rate. [Accessed 1 September 2018].

Tung, R. L. and Aycan, Z. (2008). Key success factors and indigenous management practices in SMEs in emerging economies. *Journal of World Business*, 43(4): pp. 381–384.

Tung, R. L. and Lazarova, M. (2006). Brain drain versus brain gain: An exploratory study of ex-host country nationals in central and east Europe. *The International Journal of Human Resource Management*, 17(11): pp. 1853–1872.

Upchurch, M. and Marinkovic, D. (2011). Wild capitalism, privatisation and employment relations in Serbia. *Employee Relations*, 33(4): pp. 316–333.

Vadi, M. and Vereshagin, M. V. (2006). The deposit of collectivism in organisational culture in Russia: Some consequences of human resources management. *Baltic Journal of Management*, 1(2): pp. 188–200.

Whitley, R. (1999). *Divergent Capitalisms*. Oxford: Oxford University Press.

Wilkinson, A. (1999). Employment relations in SMEs. *Employee Relations*, 21(3): pp. 206–217.

Williams, N. and Vorley, T. (2015). Institutional asymmetry: How formal and informal institutions affect entrepreneurship in Bulgaria. *International Small Business Journal*, 33(8): pp. 840–861.

Wood, G., Psychogios, A. G., Szamosi, T. L. and Collings, G. D. (2012). Institutional approaches to comparative HRM. In C. Brewster and W. Mayrhofer, eds., *Handbook of Research on Comparative Human Resource Management*. Cheltenham: Edward Elgar, pp. 27–50.

World Bank (2013). *World Development Indicators*. Washington, DC: World Bank.

Zientara, P. (2009). Employment of older workers in Polish SMEs: Employer attitudes and perceptions, employee motivations and expectations. *Human Resource Development International*, 12(2): pp. 135–153.

Zupan, N. and Kase, R. (2005). Strategic human resource management in European transition economies: Building a conceptual model on the case of Slovenia. *International Journal of Human Resource Management*, 16, pp. 882–906.

7 Challenges for SMEs in European Economic Crisis Contexts

Introduction

The severe global financial crisis occurred in late 2007 and greatly impacted businesses in countries around the world (OECD, 2008). For employees, the crisis created adverse working conditions (Psychogios et al., 2015; Psychogios et al., 2017) in terms of their employment. In Europe, the severity of the impact of the crisis varied considerably between European nations (Chatrakul Na Ayudhya et al., 2017). For example, according to Eurofound (2013a), the economic effect of the crisis in Germany, Austria, Belgium, Sweden and France was weaker in comparison with the effect the crisis had in Italy, Spain and Greece. Germany experienced some of the weaker effects, while Greece experienced the strongest effects among EU member states. National responses to the crisis, in terms of austerity cuts, also varied (Bach and Bordogna, 2013). For example, South European countries implemented the largest austerity cuts with negative implications for employment and working conditions (Eurofound, 2013b). Nations with stronger institutional bases in terms of employment policies, employment protection, industrial relations and social protection (e.g. France and Germany) implemented labour market policies that protected employment during the crisis (Gennard, 2009).

Almost a decade after the global financial crisis, global recovery is reported by media as 'broad-based and stable' (Tetlow, 2017) while some research is talking about a 'post-crisis' period (Kornelakis et al., 2017). Some advanced EU countries, such as Austria, Belgium, Germany and the Netherlands, are reported as having returned to their pre-crisis levels by 2015 (Antoshin et al., 2017). For example, Germany's GDP growth reached a six-year high of 2.2% in 2017, driven by strong private consumption, higher investment and growing foreign demand (European Commission, 2018a). However, recovery has not been experienced at the same rate by all economies and by all businesses. The impact on SMEs seems to be substantial, as they needed to adjust drastically their operations in order to survive. Without any doubt, this affected their people management strategies and practices.

The purpose of this chapter, therefore, is to explore the impact of the economic crisis on SMEs and on people management within them. The chapter will also present information from some of the European contexts hit most by the economic crisis. We focus on Greece, Italy and Spain because they experienced stronger economic effects of the crisis and implications for the general population in comparison with other EU member states (Eurofound, 2013a). For example, in Southern European countries, where social protection systems are weak, there were observable increases in inequality among families, poverty in families with children and changes in the labour and economic situation of families with children (Moreno and Mari-Klose, 2014). Another example relates to the observable decline in male-breadwinner households in Greece and Spain and the increase in female main earners. Research by Sani (2018) found these changes to come with a decrease in dual-earner households and an increase in no-earner households, suggesting negative consequences of the crisis on work-family arrangements. Sani (2018) notes that it is likely that increases in male unemployment led to reductions in dual-earner and male-breadwinner households to the advantage of no-earner households and likely poorer female-main-earner households. These two examples indicate, therefore, wider societal implications of the crisis.

Impact of Economic Crisis on European SMEs

SMEs are hugely important for the European economy. They stimulate economic growth, innovation, job creation and social integration. They represent 99% of all EU businesses, responsible for creating around 85% of new jobs in the past five years and providing two-thirds of the total private sector employment in the EU (European Commission, 2018c). Yet the economic crisis significantly affected SMEs, particularly those based in South Europe. For example, 58% of Greek SMEs were affected through insufficient working capital and 55% of them through insufficient sales (OECD, 2009). In Italy, retail trade volume fell by 4.9% in December 2008 compared to 2007, and industrial orders in manufacturing fell by 13.1% in December 2008 compared to the same period of 2007 (OECD, 2009).

Research by Lai et al. (2016) found that SMEs are more vulnerable during times of economic crisis than larger firms due to a weak resource base in terms of financial capital, human capital, HR expertise, network and market power, and this enables them to possess less discretion and options than larger organisations over strategic choices and responses during recession. SMEs are generally more vulnerable in times of crisis for a variety of reasons: inability to downsize, as they are already small; less diversification in their economic activities; weaker financial structure; lower or no credit rating; heavy dependence on credit; and fewer financing options (OECD, 2009). SMEs in value chains are even more vulnerable as they often bear the impact of the difficulties experienced by larger firms (OECD, 2009).

However, there is a debate around the topic of SME vulnerability versus resilience in times of economic turbulence. Smallbone et al. (2012) identify two broad views with respect to how firms are affected by recession. On the one hand, in the vulnerability view, SMEs are perceived to be more vulnerable to external economic shocks due to a number of size-related characteristics, such as limited financial resources, narrow customer base and product lines and less bargaining power with external stakeholders, including with finance providers. SMEs experience a tightening of the credit market, and this influences their capabilities to respond to crisis. On the other hand, the resilience view stresses that SME flexibility and adaptability may enable them to survive, or even to grow, during crisis periods. It has been argued that SMEs are flexible in terms of adjusting resource inputs, processes, prices and outputs (Reid, 2007). For example, UK small firms have been found to exhibit a strong level of resilience, flexibility, adaptability and absorptive capacity in recessions (Price et al., 2013). However, this is not the case across all EU SMEs.

Research by Beck and Demirguc-Kunt (2006) suggests that SMEs use external finance, but they are significantly constrained in obtaining it in comparison with larger firms, a problem which has been exacerbated by the recent crisis (OECD, 2009). In 2015, 30% of EU-28 SMEs had applied for credit line, bank overdraft or credit line overdraft, 28% for a bank loan, 35% for trade credit and 16% for other forms of external funding (European Commission, 2015c). However, access to finance is the most important concern for 10% of EU SMEs (European Commission, 2015a).

The financial crisis further exacerbated the problem of access to finance for SMEs (Psillaki and Eleftheriou, 2015) particularly for South European SMEs. In Greece, 30% of SMEs reported that access to finance was their most significant problem, with a worsening in the availability of bank loans due to their declining turnovers and unusual levels of liquid assets over the crisis period (European Central Bank, 2016). In Spain, 80% of SMEs seeking a bank credit in 2008 experienced problems in obtaining one: the amounts offered by banks in 59% of the cases were lower than requested by their clients, and in 26%, the credit horizon had been reduced by the bank (OECD, 2009). In Italy, 87% of SMEs reported a tightening in credit standards in 2008 (OECD, 2009). This difficulty in accessing finance led to corporate insolvencies. For example, Italy and Ireland reported more than 25% of businesses becoming insolvent in 2008/2009 (OECD, 2009).

In addition, research by Casey and O'Toole (2014) focuses specifically on EU SMEs and explores whether bank lending constraints in times of crisis increase firm demand for alternative forms of external finance. Their study covers the 2009–2011 crisis period. They suggest that the financial crisis significantly constrained bank credit to SMEs across the EU. The highest levels were observed in Greek, Irish and Spanish SMEs. Such credit-rationed firms were denied finance from banks or received less finance than the amount sought. In the case of Greek SMEs, they turned to increased usage of trade credit (credit extended by the suppliers) and market financing and exhibited one of the highest percentages of reported usage of these financing mechanisms in comparison with other EU states. However, given the significant impact of the crisis on the entire Greek economy, a vicious circle of trade credit between suppliers was created, therefore not making this a very effective method of SME financing. For example, many SMEs act as suppliers/creditors to larger companies (OECD, 2009), increasing their vulnerability of foreclosure. A recent example: one of the biggest supermarkets in Greece (Carrefur-Marinopoulos) had 2,500–3,000 suppliers/creditors. These suppliers experienced cash flow problems (delayed and partial payment for services rendered or goods delivered). In the final discussions for saving the company, it was decided that they would forfeit 50% of the value of all outstanding invoices. The original proposal stated that they would pay the remaining 50% in 15 years, a financially devastating decision for SMEs acting as their suppliers. Overall, SMEs in Croatia, Cyprus, Greece, Italy, Portugal and Spain recorded a decline in number of SME enterprises, level of SME employment and SME value added in the 2008–2016 period (European Commission, 2016a).

Therefore, SMEs have financing obstacles in comparison with larger organisations and these are caused by factors such as size, age and ownership of the firm (Beck and Demirguc-Kunt, 2006) in addition to the underdevelopment of financial institutions in some contexts (e.g. banks, investment funds, insurance and pension funds, stock exchange, bond market) (European Commission, 2015b). The economic crisis has further exacerbated the problem of access to finance for SMEs, particularly in the South European periphery (Psillaki and Eleftheriou, 2015).

Finally, the global financial crisis has undermined the foundations of organisational trust that contributes to national economic growth and socio-economic development at the macro level, and entrepreneurship and business development at the micro level (Altinay et al., 2014), thus impacting organisational trust. We know that the economic crisis has undermined both organisational and individual trust at their most fundamental level (Gounaris and Prout, 2009). National crises are, above all, trust crises (Bachmann and Inkpen, 2011), as societal perceptions change, and whether accurate or not, those who were once considered trustworthy may no longer be viewed as such (Fulmer and Gelfand, 2012). This is particularly the case for SMEs, where national crises raise additional fears of supply or payment (Barron et al., 2015). It is clear that crises do break organisational trust (Gounaris and Prout, 2009). As a result, SMEs are forced to directly address a trust gap in their relations with both internal and external stakeholders. Due to reductions in, or the outright loss of, stakeholder trust, goal attainment and mission accomplishment are threatened. This highlights the importance of trust repair as a critical managerial competency and a matter of survival (Gillespie and Dietz, 2009).

Impact of Economic Crisis on Managing People

During the economic crisis, organisational agility, through scalable workforce, fast organisational learning and a highly adaptable organisational infrastructure, was essential for survival in this dynamic and unpredictable environment (Nijssen and Paauwe, 2012). Many organisations had to respond by cutting labour costs, either by reducing recruitment, implementing pay cuts, restructuring, downsizing or instituting layoffs (Iverson and Zatzick, 2011; Naude et al., 2012). The methods that companies use to respond to crisis can be classified into three aspects: wage adjustment; workforce adjustment; and redesign of working methods (Roche et al., 2011). Wage adjustment refers to cutting of various compensation policies like basic salaries, bonuses, etc. Workforce adjustment relates to organisational downsizing, layoffs, early retirement, etc. Work redesign is associated with flexible forms of work, including short-term work, part-time and/or temporary work, etc. It seems though that the situation in SMEs is even more problematic due to their 'sensitive' nature. In other words, the lack of robust HR practices in combination with the negative outcomes of crisis on businesses may result in the adoption of more extreme measures by management (Psychogios et al., 2017). The fact that SMEs are less likely to be unionised provides greater opportunities to make labour-related cost savings during recession (Lai et al., 2016).

As a result, employees in SMEs have to deal with an increase in job insecurity, work intensification and pressure (Chung and Van Oorschot, 2011; Datta et al., 2010; Mellahi and Wilkinson, 2008; Psychogios et al., 2015; Prouska and Psychogios, 2018a,b; Russell and McGinnity, 2014). These deteriorating working conditions have been reported to affect employee physical and mental health and well-being (Maslach and Leiter, 2008; Rosen et al., 2012). For example, research by Buss (2009) has linked the economic crisis and the accompanying changes in the nature of employment to an increase in depression, anxiety and alcohol-related disorders. In addition, research by Shoss and Probst (2012) found that both stressors and stress-related sickness absence significantly increased during the 2008 economic crisis.

Furthermore, the economic crisis has had an effect on employee motivation, commitment, productivity and loyalty as many organisations reduced the number of opportunities for training and development, rewards and career advancement (Allen et al., 2001; Kalimo et al., 2003; McDonnell and Burgess, 2013; Spreitzer and Mishra, 2002). Research has found that prosocial behaviours at work (voluntary actions that are intended to help or benefit the workplace) diminish during austerity times (Shoss and Probst, 2012), as employees are preoccupied with their own personal economic situation and their capability to keep their jobs and their rewards (Giorgi et al., 2015). As a result, employees might develop job dissatisfaction and psychological distress resulting from a fear of the implications the economic crisis may have on their job (Giorgi et al., 2015).

Finally, it seems that the economic crisis influenced development and talent management practices of SMEs. Sharmila and Gopalakrishnan (2013) state that in the period of the global economic crisis, the topic of talent management has become important for SMEs, particularly how to retain talented employees in an unstable economic environment. Such circumstances provide a great opportunity for organisations to use a talent management system that should optimise employee performance and improve their skills to manage various complex tasks. However, Stokes et al. (2016) confirm that certain studies state that only 5% of SMEs operating in crisis contexts have a defined talent management strategy. This is a major operational problem when the use and development of talents are at stake. Borisova et al. (2017) argue that SMEs that have introduced a talent management strategy have significantly shifted the HRM responsibilities for employees to all executives in the organisation and, thus, created an effective talent network that could respond more effectively to the challenges of crisis.

Overall, economic crises seem to have a drastic impact on managing people in SMEs. In particular, there is evidence suggesting that crises have a negative impact on employee motivation, commitment, job satisfaction, trust towards management and their performance. The next three sections explore three crisis contexts: Greece, Italy and Spain. The discussion focuses on the impact of the economic crisis on business, employment, labour and market conditions.

Greece

The profound effects the recent crisis had on various aspects of Greece's political, social and economic life has attracted a lot of academic and practitioner research. The economic crisis in Greece led to both endogenous and exogenous institutional change (Williams and Vorley, 2015). Greek institutions are traditionally weak (Prouska and Kapsali, 2011; Psychogios and Wood, 2010). The crisis has made them more dysfunctional in terms of regulating labour markets and securing viable and sustainable growth (Kornelakis and Voskeristian, 2014).

Since 2009, Greece has been experiencing a decline in wages and an increase in part-time and fixed-term employment, resulting in increased job insecurity according to the European Job Quality Index (Leschke et al., 2012). Greece experienced a negative GDP growth of –0.2% in 2016, although real GDP was expected to reach 1.6% in 2017 (European Commission, 2018b). Greece received three bailouts for a total of EUR 246 billion and implemented harsh austerity measures which generated chronic high unemployment, widespread poverty and plummeting incomes, while real GDP contracted by approximately one-fourth between 2009 and 2015 (Kindreich, 2017). Gross public debt stood at 185% of GDP in 2016, GDP growth at –0.7%, inflation at 0.5%, and unemployment at 24% (European Commission, 2016b). As a result, the Greek economy almost collapsed because of the economic crisis. The austerity measures implemented had a critical impact on the labour force, particularly among younger workers (Psychogios et al., 2016). Greece experienced a 22% increase in job insecurity during the crisis (2007–2012) compared to an EU-27 average of 4% (Eurofound, 2016). At the same time, Greece had reduced its minimum wage by 22% since 2008, the highest cut in the EU (Eurofound, 2016).

The crisis had a significant impact on the levels of social inequality and poverty in Greece. Research by Andriopoulou et al. (2017) during the 2007–2014 period found that there was a decline in the income shares of the two lowest and the top decile of the population. Relative poverty recorded a substantial increase. They note that, taking into account that disposable income declined by almost 40% in the period under examination, it is not surprising to find that the estimated poverty indices rose between 100% and 200% in that period.

The effects of the economic crisis have been critically negative for many Greek companies (Arghyrou and Tsoukalas, 2010), especially SMEs (OECD, 2016a). These firms had to overcome increased taxation but also cope with the inability of the country's banks to support them financially. In addition, a significant number of SMEs had liquidity problems, being unable in many cases to pay their suppliers and employees (Kouretas and Vlamis, 2010). This problem intensified in June 2015 when capital controls were implemented in an effort to stop a likely bank run due to the political instability in the country (Samitas and Polyzos, 2016). Moreover, increased layoffs and decreased salaries have led to high uncertainty and employee dissatisfaction, especially within SMEs (Arghyrou and Tsoukalas, 2010).

Moreover, the crisis created a trust gap in businesses including SMEs, making the crisis structural (Wood et al., 2015). The prevailing structural crisis in Greece has increased the possibility of organisation-stakeholder trust failures. Thus, repairing such trust under weak or unstable economic conditions is even more arduous given the prevailing greater sense of uncertainty (Prout, 2009).

Furthermore, since 2011, a rapid decentralisation of collective bargaining to enterprise level and a decrease in the number of labour market regulations deriving from sector-level and occupational collective employment agreements have been observed and attributed to the economic crisis (Ioannou and Papadimitriou, 2013). In the past, Greek trade unions were considered a politicised form of employee representation with strong confrontational and militant strategies, hence making employment relations highly conflictual in collective negotiations (Mihail, 2004).

However, since 2009, there has been a decline in trade unionism with an evident relaxation in the strictness of employment protection for regular contracts, temporary contracts and dismissals (OECD, 2016b). Although unions are the most important form of employee representation, the law also provides for works council structures. These are only found in a few companies, and where they exist, they work closely with the local union, while where there is no union in place, there will not be a works council (ETUI, 2016). The crisis also resulted in the emergence of 'associations of persons'. A 2011 law enables these associations to operate without a time limitation and with the authority to sign collective agreements for companies of any size, provided that (i) there is no union in place and (ii) 60% of the workforce are members of the association (ETUI, 2016). However, representatives of these associations have no permanent mandate and no protection against mistreatment by the employer. Although collective action is moderately high (Wallace and O'Sullivan, 2006), employees in smaller enterprises do not often have this collective avenue for expressing voice (Kouzis, 2000).

Research by Wood et al. (2015) explored changes in industrial relations regulation and practice in the Greek context. They argue that Greek industrial relations have undergone a long process of deregulation that has been accelerated since the onset of the economic crisis and the inherent segmentation of the Greek system between regulated players and largely unregulated informal and SME players. Radical neo-liberal reforms have weakened the position of larger formal sector employers and employees who are most reliant on traditional regulatory arrangements. This has made the basis of Greek competitiveness more fragile.

Within this context, some research has also focused on studying employee silence in SMEs within the Greek long-term economic crisis context (Prouska and Psychogios, 2018a, b). More specifically, we (Prouska and Psychogios, 2018a) explored how employee silence is formulated in long-term turbulent economic environments and in more vulnerable organisational settings, such as in SMEs. The study drew on qualitative data gathered from 63 interviews with employees in a total of 48 small enterprises in Greece in two periods of time (2009 and 2015). The authors suggest a new type of employee silence, *social empathy silence*, and offer a conceptual framework for understanding the development of silence over time in particular contexts of long-term turbulence and crisis. In addition, a second study by Prouska and Psychogios (2018b) explored line managers' experience of voice and silence from their own perspective and organisational position. This study drew on qualitative data gathered from line managers in 35 small non-unionised enterprises in Greece in two periods of time (2012 and 2014) during the economic crisis. The authors develop a framework for understanding line managers' experience of silence in such contexts and, within this framework, propose *cynical silence* as a new type of silence relevant to an economic crisis context. This research on employee silence highlights the effects of the economic crisis on employees and managers and raises questions about employee voice at work during economic turbulent times.

Italy

Italy is another example of a South European country affected by the recent crisis. The economic crisis of 2008 hit Italy just as Prodi's government collapsed and Berlusconi and the Right regained power (Pasquino, 2008). Italy had been in political instability since 2000, when coalitions of both the Right and Left had been in office, but neither proved capable of stopping the political unrest and economic decline (Di Quirico, 2010). Up until the 2008 crisis, growth and growth prospects remained limited, while employment policies were designed around temporary work resulting in low wages and a decline in workers' rights.

Therefore, when the crisis hit in 2008, it hit an already vulnerable institutional setting. Italy already had deep-rooted structural problems that resulted in unsatisfactory productivity performance and growth over the last two decades (Morsy and Sgherri, 2010). The crisis exacerbated these long-term weaknesses. By 2009, a 5.5% drop in GDP was observed as well as a fall in manufacturing output of 16.6% (Regalia and Regini, 2018). The crisis also affected Italy's main trading partners, and this led to a sharp fall in exports, while private consumption declined due to tighter consumer credit and the uncertainty over economic conditions (Morsy and Sgherri, 2010).

At the same time, the crisis increased the risk of poverty; 18.2% of residents in Italy were at risk of poverty at the peak of the crisis (2007–2009), while 6.9% lived in conditions of severe material deprivation (Borghi, 2013). Italian families were squeezed by increased tax burdens and cuts in social and health spending, all of which increased the risk of poverty among Italian families (Borghi, 2013).

Italian banks had to reduce credit to clients and raise the amount of collateral required for new loans. This affected SMEs that heavily relied on bank credit (Casey and O'Toole, 2014) but also consumers, who were deterred from spending as a result of these credit restrictions. Microenterprises suffered the most in this respect. Given the importance of SMEs for the Italian economy (99.99% of all enterprises are SMEs, and they account for nearly 80% of the industrial and service labour force), this restriction in accessing finance led to 50,000 businesses closing between 2008 and 2013, bankruptcies nearly doubling and reaching a total of 104,000 in 2012, the total unemployment rate jumping from 6.7% to 12.1% and value added decreasing by 5% for SMEs (Salimi, 2015).

The recovery plan implemented by the government included a bonus for low-income families in the form of a tax credit, and for companies, tax deductions and an increase in the funds for technical unemployment (Hodorogel, 2009). Italy has received several economic bailout programmes from Germany during the crisis, as well as injections of money in the market by the executive in Rome. The bailout programmes came with conditions, such as reducing employees' health insurance payments and cutting the salary tax (first taxation level) (Hodorogel, 2009).

SMEs represent approximately 95% of the Italian economy and provide around 50% of its employment (Eurofound, 2010a). The Bank of Italy estimated that, in 2009, the recession has had the greatest impact on small companies in terms of turnover, profitability, investments and employment (Eurofound, 2010a). SMEs either had to downsize due to a lack of sales or shut down operations (Giorgi et al., 2015). The result was that sectors such as real estate, housebuilding and car manufacturing collapsed (Bugamelli et al., 2009). Larger firms had to internalise almost all of the production processes with damaging effects for their subcontractors and suppliers (Eurofound, 2010a). They also had to delay payments to suppliers and negotiate lower prices, therefore putting more financial pressure on SMEs, who had to now bear the cost of the crisis (Bugamelli et al., 2009). As a result, at the end of 2009, the lowest rate of small enterprise creation was recorded since 2003 (at 0.28% growth compared with the previous year), while closures increased by 3.7% compared to 2008 (Eurofound, 2010a). SMEs struggled for survival due to their difficulty in securing credit, the fewer resources available to undertake reorganisation, and the difficulties experienced by larger organisations to which SMEs acted as suppliers (Eurofound, 2010a).

The crisis led to an unstable economy and an increase in unemployment, particularly for younger workers (Choudhry et al., 2012). Unemployment rates grew from 6.7% in 2008 to 11.7% in 2016, but unemployment rates among the young cohort grew from 21.2% in 2008 to 37.8% in 2016 (Regalia and Regini, 2018). This fear of unemployment in Italian firms during the economic crisis increased employees' psychological distress and decreased their job satisfaction (Giorgi et al., 2015).

Within this context, the role of trade unions was seen as increasingly important. However, in the decade prior to the crisis, Italian trade unions had experienced a decline in power due to decentralisation and a gradual loss of economic and political influence. During the crisis, trade unions showed an unexpected resilience; union density increased during the crisis and their position as key actors of Italian economic and political life was strengthened (Regalia and Regini, 2018). This is explained by the fact that Italian trade unions had, over the years, become involved in a variety of social and public policy spheres, and this made it difficult for any government to ignore or to openly confront them. This does not mean, however, that not much has changed in industrial relations during the years of the crisis. In fact, the crisis brought many changes, such as the increased ability of governments to intervene in the labour market. Successive measures have altered redundancy protection for workers, reduced the wage guarantee fund, made unemployment benefits almost universal, relaxed the regulations on work contracts to facilitate hiring and improved the work/family reconciliation policy to encourage female employment (Regalia and Regini, 2018).

In relation to the effect of the crisis on the HR managers' role in Italy, Boldizzoni and Quarantino (2011) conducted a survey in 102 large companies. This research found that the crisis has contributed to a slowdown in the adoption of roles focused on investing in people and organisational development.

Spain

Spain is another interesting example to study in relation to how the crisis has affected business, market and labour conditions. The Spanish economy has been much affected by the global economic crisis, as the imbalances accumulated in the boom period prior to the crisis made Spain vulnerable to changes in macroeconomic and financial conditions (Ortega and Penalosa, 2012). Spain's vulnerability to the crisis was determined by the high external debt and the level of household indebtedness, by the relatively low labour productivity and by the fact that the economy depended mainly on small enterprises (Eurofound, 2010b); 87% of employees work in SMEs, with 42% employed in microenterprises (Eurofound, 2011b). The most affected SME sector in Spain was the construction sector, with an estimated 20% in job losses since 2008 (Eurofound, 2011a).

Research by Carballo-Cruz (2011) found that in 2011, non-financial firms' debt, in terms of gross operating surplus, was around 750%, surpassing those of the Eurozone (550%), the UK (650%) and the US (350%). This piece of research notes considerable differences at the sectoral level. For example, the construction and property development sectors are the worst hit sectors in this respect due to the enormous stock of unsold real estate assets.

By 2012, overall unemployment in Spain reached 24.8% (European Commission, 2018d) with youth unemployment at 53.2% (European Commission, 2018e). The unemployment rate in 2018 shows some improvement and currently stands at 16.7%, with youth unemployment at 33.8%. (Trading Economics, 2018a, b). Historically, Spain has faced unemployment challenges. Attempts to address these challenges have been made since the 1980s through a range of flexibility reforms (Banyuls et al., 2009). However, these attempts have created an employment model that is highly sensitive to economic cycles (Muñoz de Bustillo and Antón, 2012) and highly segmented, with especially unstable groups in the labour market (Bernardi and Martínez-Pastor, 2010). These unstable groups are composed of workers in unskilled services and construction, particularly young people, immigrants and women (Lopez-Andreu and Verd, 2016). These groups benefited from measures to increase their participation in the labour market during the 1996–2007 period but were also affected by the spectacular job losses that occurred thereafter (ILO, 2011).

Unemployment, therefore, particularly affected young and female workers and those with a low educational level (Casado et al., 2012). This trend had a direct effect on the evolution of intergenerational occupational mobility. Mobility has increased as a whole, but downward occupational mobility has increased for the unemployed during the economic crisis, meaning that the crisis has made disadvantaged groups more vulnerable in terms of employment (Ruiz, 2018).

The high unemployment deteriorated family income and, consequently, put pressure on the Spanish welfare state. Research by Moreno (2017) found that high unemployment and precarious jobs negatively affected household income and increased the risk of poverty or social exclusion. This research found that inequality increased and available income decreased after 2008, and this trend was particularly strong after 2010. In addition, income decreased more significantly in the lowest income bracket, therefore affecting the most vulnerable segments of the population. Growing inequalities were also found in employment and wages of people with disabilities during the crisis (Garrido-Cumbrera and Chacon-Garcia, 2018). Such increasing inequality is particularly evident in Spain, in contrast with the more moderate growth of inequality in Germany and Sweden, which may be attributable to the cushion effect of their social policies (Moreno, 2017).

The Spanish labour market is characterised by low flexibility, reduced employment security, low internal mobility and wage rigidities, while trade social protection expenditure is high, employment protection legislation is stiff and early retirement exhibits high levels (Aceleanu, 2013). For those in employment, the economic crisis raised labour instability, lowered wages and increased workloads with a direct impact on job satisfaction (Sanchez-Sellero and Sanchez-Sellero, 2017).

Training and development opportunities were also affected. There was a 30% reduction of national funds made available for the national training system, which drastically affected the number of participants trained (from 54% in 2004 to 7% in 2013) (Rigby and Sanz, 2016). Spain is lacking in training and development in comparison with other EU countries. Any progress made in the decade after the introduction of the national training system in 1992 was threatened by the economic crisis, which negatively affected training spend per worker and training budgets (Rigby and Sanz, 2016).

In terms of employee relations, great pressure for change was exerted through the new collective bargaining rules imposed on the social partners in February 2012. According to Eurofound (2013c), the main changes were, first, decentralisation of collective bargaining arrangements by giving preference to company agreements over multi-employer agreements, and second, new regulation allowing companies to opt out of collective bargaining if the enterprise records a drop in its revenues or sales during six consecutive months. The law also allows enterprises to modify wages on technical or organisational grounds which justify the measure.

Summary

Chapter 7 explored the challenges posed to European SMEs by the economic crisis. Many SMEs struggled for survival in increasingly turbulent markets. Their heavy dependence on credit and their inability to access finance when they needed it the most created a trade deficit between them and their suppliers, with spillover effects on employees. SMEs struggled to overcome the economic crisis due to their inability to downsize and diversify products/services, their weak financial structures and their limited access to finance. As a response to these impediments, SMEs had to cut labour costs by freezing recruitment, downsizing, implementing pay cuts and layoffs. This context led to the intensification of adverse working conditions for employees in SMEs, making their working lives prone to job insecurity, work intensification and pressure. As a result, employee productivity, loyalty and commitment exhibited a decline. SMEs need strategies to retain engagement and performance levels, particularly in order to maintain levels of employee engagement in this challenging context.

References

Aceleanu, M. I. (2013). The labour market in the post-crisis economy: The case of Spain. *Theoretical and Applied Economics*, 20(3): pp. 135–146.

Allen, D., Freeman, M., Russell, A., Reizenstein, C. and Rentz, O. (2001). Survivor reactions to organisational downsizing: Does time ease the pain? *Journal of Occupational and Organisational Psychology*, 74: pp. 145–164.

Altinay, L., Saunders, M. N. and Wang, C. L. (2014). The influence of culture on trust judgments in customer relationship development by ethnic minority small businesses. *Journal of Small Business Management*, 52(1): pp. 59–78.

Andriopoulou, E., Karakitsios, A. and Tsakloglou, P. (2017). *Inequality and poverty in Greece: Changes in times of crisis*. GreeSE Paper No.116, Hellenic Observatory on Greece and Southeast Europe, Hellenic Observatory – European Institute. [online]. Available at: http://eprints.lse.ac.uk/85329/1/GreeSE%20116.pdf.

Antoshin, S., Arena, M., Gueorguiev, N., Lybek, T., Ralyea, J. and Yehoue, E. B. (2017). *Credit growth and economic recovery in Europe after the global financial crisis*. IMF working paper WP/17/256, International Monetary Fund.

Arghyrou, M. and Tsoukalas, J. (2010). The Greek debt crisis: Likely causes, mechanics and outcomes. *The World Economy*, 34(2): pp. 173–191.

Bach, S. and Bordogna, L. (2013). Reframing public service employment relations: The impact of economic crisis and the new EU economic governance. *European Journal of Industrial Relations*, 19(4): pp. 279–294.

Bachmann, R. and Inkpen, A. (2011). Understanding institutional-based trust building processes in inter-organisational relationships. *Organisation Studies*, 32(2): pp. 281–301.

Banyuls, J., Miguélez, F., Recio, A., Cano, E. and Llorente, P. (2009). The transformation of the employment system in Spain: Towards a Mediterranean neoliberalism? In G. Bosch, S. Lehndorff and J. Rubery, eds., *European Employment Models in Flux. A Comparison of Institutional Change in Nine European Countries*. New York: Palgrave-Macmillan, pp. 247–269.

Barron, A., Hultén, P. and Vanyushyn, V. (2015). Country-of-origin effects on managers' environmental scanning behaviours: Evidence from the political crisis in the Eurozone. *Environment and Planning C: Government and Policy*, 33(3): pp. 601–619.

Beck, T. and Demirguc-Kunt, A. (2006). Small and medium-size enterprises: Access to finance as a growth constraint. *Journal of Banking and Finance*, 30(11): pp. 2931–2943.

Bernardi, F. and Martínez-Pastor, J. I. (2010). Falling at the bottom: Unskilled jobs at entry in the labour market in Spain over time and in a comparative perspective. *International Journal of Comparative Sociology*, 51(4): pp. 289–307.

Boldizzoni, D. and Quaratino, L. (2011). The role of human resource manager: Change agent vs. business partner? Research into HRM in Italy. *EBS Review*, 28: pp. 41–52.

Borghi, E. (2013). *The impact of anti-crisis measures and the social and employment situation: Italy, European economic and social committee.* [online]. Available at: www.eesc.europa.eu/resources/docs/qe-32-12-542-en-c.pdf. [Accessed 1 September 2018].

Borisova, O. N., Silayeva, A. A., Saburova, L. N., Belokhvostova, N. V. and Sokolova, A. P. (2017). Talent management as an essential element in a corporate personnel development strategy. *Academy of Strategic Management Journal*, 16(1): pp. 1631–1646.

Bugamelli, M., Cristadoro, R. and Zevi, G. (2009). *La crisi internazionale e il sistema produttivo italiano: Un'analisi su dati a livello di impresa, occasional papers 58*. Rome: Banca d'Italia.

Buss, P. M. (2009). Public health and the world economic crisis. *Journal of Epidemiology and Community Health*, 63: p. 417.

Carballo-Cruz, F. (2011). Causes and consequences of the Spanish economic crisis: Why the recovery is taken so long? *Panoeconomicus*, 3: pp. 309–328.

Casado, J. M., Fernández-Vidaurreta, C. and Jimeno, J. F. (2012, January). *Labour Flows in the EU at the Beginning of the Crisis*. Spain: Banco De España-Economic Bulletin.

Casey, E. and O'Toole, C. M. (2014). Bank lending constraints, trade credit and alternative financing during the financial crisis: Evidence from European SMEs. *Journal of Corporate Finance*, 27: pp. 173–193.

Chatrakul Na Ayudhya, U., Prouska, R. and Beauregard, A. (2017). The impact of global economic crisis and austerity on quality of working life and work-life balance: A capabilities perspective. *European Management Review*. First published 17 July 2017. doi:10.1111/emre.12128.

Choudhry, M. T., Marelli, E. and Signorelli, M. (2012). Youth unemployment rate and impact of financial crises. *International Journal of Manpower*, 33: pp. 76–95.

Chung, H. and Van Oorschot, W. (2011). Institutions versus market forces: Explaining the employment insecurity of European individuals during (the beginning of) the financial crisis. *Journal of European Social Policy*, 21(4): pp. 287–301.

Datta, K., Guthrie, P., Basuil, D. and Pandey, A. (2010). Causes and effects of employee downsizing: A review and synthesis. *Journal of Management*, 36: pp. 281–348.

Di Quirico, R. (2010). Italy and the global economic crisis. *Bulletin of Italian Politics*, 2(2): pp. 3–19.

ETUI (2016). *Greece - workplace representation*. [online]. Available at: www.worker-participation.eu/National-Industrial-Relations/Countries/Greece/Workplace-Representation. [Accessed 17 April 2016].

Eurofound (2010a). *Effects of economic crisis on Italian economy*. [online]. Available at: www.eurofound.europa.eu/observatories/eurwork/articles/effects-of-economic-crisis-on-italian-economy. [Accessed 1 September 2018].

Eurofound (2010b). *Spain: A country profile*. [online]. Available at: www.eurofound.europa.eu/publications/report/2010/spain/working-conditions-quality-of-life/spain-a-country-profile. [Accessed 29 June 2018].

Eurofound (2011a). *Final questionnaire for EIRO CAR on SMEs in the crisis: Employment, industrial relations and local partnership*. [online]. Available at: www.eurofound.europa.eu/observatories/eurwork/comparative-information/national-contributions/spain/final-questionnaire-for-eiro-car-on-smes-in-the-crisis-employment-industrial-relations-and-local. [Accessed 29 June 2018].

Eurofound (2011b). *SMEs in the crisis: Employment, industrial relations and local partnership*. [online]. Available at: www.eurofound.europa.eu/observatories/

eurwork/comparative-information/smes-in-the-crisis-employment-industrial-relations-and-local-partnership. [Accessed 29 June 2018].

Eurofound (2013a). *Impact of the crisis on working conditions: Technical annex.* [online]. Available at: www.eurofound.europa.eu/sites/default/files/ef_files/docs/ewco/tn1212025s/tn1212025s_technical_annex.pdf. [Accessed 6 April 2018].

Eurofound (2013b). *Impact of the crisis on working conditions in Europe.* [online]. Available at: www.eurofound.europa.eu/sites/default/files/ef_files/docs/ewco/tn1212025s/tn1212025s.pdf. [Accessed 6 April 2018].

Eurofound (2013c). *Spain: Impact of the crisis on industrial relations.* [online]. Available at: www.eurofound.europa.eu/publications/report/2013/spain-impact-of-the-crisis-on-industrial-relations. [Accessed 1 September 2018].

Eurofound (2016). *Impact of the crisis on working conditions in Europe – Impact on employment conditions.* [online]. Available at: www.eurofound.europa.eu/observatories/eurwork/comparative-information/impact-of-the-crisis-on-working-conditions-in-europe. [Accessed 13 March 2016].

European Central Bank (2016). *Survey on the access to finance of enterprises in the Euro area: October 2015 to March 2016.* [online]. Available at: www.ecb.europa.eu/pub/pdf/other/accesstofinancesmallmediumsizedenterprises201606.en.pdf?c96d449e601cbe6c87d2e67d54e68c70. [Accessed 1 September 2018].

European Commission (2015a). *European semester thematic factsheet: Small and medium sized enterprises.* [online]. Available at: https://ec.europa.eu/info/sites/info/files/european-semester_thematic-factsheet_small-medium-enterprises-access-finance_en.pdf.

European Commission (2015b). *Small and medium-sized enterprises' access to finance.* European semester thematic fiche. [online]. Available at: http://ec.europa.eu/europe2020/pdf/themes/2015/small_medium_enterprises_access_to_finance_20151126.pdf.

European Commission (2015c). *Survey on the access to finance of enterprises (SAFE): Analytical report 2015.* Directorate-General for Internal Market, Industry, Entrepreneurship and SMEs.

European Commission (2016a). *Annual report on European SMEs 2016/17: Focus on self-employment.* [online]. Available at: https://ec.europa.eu/growth/smes/business-friendly-environment/performance-review_en#annual-report. [Accessed 29 June 2018].

European Commission (2016b). *Greece – economic outlook.* [online]. Available at: http://ec.europa.eu/economy_finance/eu/countries/greece_en.htm. [Accessed 28 March 2016].

European Commission (2018a). *Economic forecast for Germany.* [online]. Available at: https://ec.europa.eu/info/business-economy-euro/economic-performance-and-forecasts/economic-performance-country/germany/economic-forecast-germany_en. [Accessed 6 April 2018].

European Commission (2018b). *Economic forecast for Greece.* [online]. Available at: https://ec.europa.eu/info/business-economy-euro/economic-performance-and-forecasts/economic-performance-country/greece/economic-forecast-greece_en. [Accessed 6 April 2018].

European Commission (2018c). *Entrepreneurship and small and medium-sized enterprises (SMEs).* [online]. Available at: https://ec.europa.eu/growth/smes_en. [Accessed 6 April 2018].

European Commission (2018d). *Unemployment statistics.* [online]. Available at: http://ec.europa.eu/eurostat/statistics-explained/index.php/Unemployment_statistics#Longer-term_unemployment_trends. [Accessed 6 June 2018].

European Commission (2018e). *Youth unemployment.* [online]. Available at: http://ec.europa.eu/eurostat/statistics-explained/index.php/Youth_unemployment. [Accessed 6 June 2018].

Fulmer, C. and Gelfand, M. J. (2012). At what level (and in whom) we trust: Trust across multiple organisational levels. *Journal of Management*, 38(4): pp. 1167–1230.

Garrido-Cumbrera, M. and Chacon-Garcia, J. (2018). Assessing the impact of the 2008 financial crisis on the labour force, employment, and wages of persons with disabilities in Spain. *Journal of Disability Policy Studies*, p. 11. doi:10.1177/1044207318776437.

Gennard, J. (2009). The financial crisis and employee relations. *Employee Relations*, 31(5): pp. 451–454.

Gillespie, N. and Dietz, G. (2009). Trust repair after an organisation-level failure. *Academy of Management Review*, 34(1): pp. 127–145.

Giorgi, G., Shoss, M. K. and Leon-Perez, J. (2015). Going beyond workplace stressors: Economic crisis and perceived employability in relation to psychological distress and job dissatisfaction. *International Journal of Stress Management*, 22(2): pp. 137–158.

Gounaris, K. and Prout, M. (2009). Repairing relationships and restoring trust: Behavioural finance and the economic crisis. *Journal of Financial Service Professionals*, 63(4): pp. 75–84.

Hodorogel, R. (2009). The economic crisis and its effects on SMEs. *Theoretical and Applied Economics*, 5(534): pp. 79–88.

ILO (2011). *Spain: Quality Jobs for a new Economy.* Geneva: ILO Publications.

Ioannou, C. and Papadimitriou, K. (2013). *Collective Bargaining in Greece in 2011 and 2012: Trends, Breakthroughs and Prospects (in Greek).* Athens: OMED (Organisation for Mediation and Arbitration).

Iverson, R. and Zatzick, C. (2011). The effects of downsizing on labour productivity: The value of showing consideration for employees' moral and welfare in high-performance work systems. *Human Resource Management*, 50(1): pp. 29–44.

Kalimo, R., Taris, T. and Schaufeli, W. (2003). The effects of past and anticipated future downsizing on survivor well-being: An equity perspective. *Journal of Occupational Health Psychology*, 8(2): pp. 91–109.

Kindreich, A. (2017). *The Greek financial crisis (2009–2016).* [online]. Available at: www.econcrises.org/2017/07/20/the-greek-financial-crisis-2009-2016/. [Accessed 6 April 2018].

Kornelakis, A. and Voskeristian, H. (2014). The transformation of employment regulation in Greece: Towards a dysfunctional liberal market economy? *Relations Industrielles/Industrial Relations Quarterly Review*, 69(2): pp. 344–365. doi:10.7202/1025032ar.

Kornelakis, A., Veliziotis, M. and Voskeritsian, H. (2017). How can competitiveness be achieved in post-crisis Europe? Deregulating employment relations or enhancing high performance work practices? *The International Journal of Human Resource Management*, 28(21): pp. 2957–2976.

Kouretas, G. and Vlamis, P. (2010). The Greek crisis: Causes and implications. *Panoeconomicus*, 57(4): pp. 391–404. doi:10.2298/PAN1004391K.

Kouzis, Y. (2000). The impact of EMU on labor relations. *Επιθεώρηση Εργασιακών Σχέσεων* (in Greek), 18: pp. 57–66.

Lai, Y., Saridakis, G., Blackburn, R. and Johnstone, S. (2016). Are the HR responses of small firms different from large firms in times of recession? *Journal of Business Venturing*, 31(1): pp. 113–131.

Leschke, J., Watt, A. and Finn, M. (2012). *Job Quality in the Crisis – An Update of the Job Quality Index (JQI)*. Brussels: European Trade Institute.

Lopez-Andreu, M. and Verd, J. M. (2016). Employment instability and economic crisis in Spain: What are the elements that make a difference in the trajectories of younger adults? *European Societies*, 18(4): pp. 315–335.

Maslach, C. and Leiter, M. P. (2008). Early predictors of job burnout and engagement. *Journal of Applied Psychology*, 93: pp. 498–512.

McDonnell, A. and Burgess, J. (2013). The impact of the global financial crisis on managing employees. *International Journal of Manpower*, 34: pp. 184–197.

Mellahi, K. and Wilkinson, A. (2008). A study of the association between downsizing and innovation determinants. *International Journal of Innovation Management*, 12: pp. 677–698.

Mihail, D. M. (2004). Labour flexibility in Greek SMEs. *Personnel Review*, 33(5): pp. 549–560.

Moreno, A. M. (2017). Understanding the impact of economic crisis on inequality, household structure, and family support in Spain from a comparative perspective. *Journal of Poverty*, 21(5): pp. 454–481.

Moreno, L. and Mari-Klose, P. (2013). Youth, family change and welfare arrangements. *European Societies*, 15(4): pp. 493–513.

Morsy, H. and Sgherri, S. (2010). *After the crisis: Assessing the damage in Italy*. IMF Working Paper WP/10/244. [online]. Available at: www.imf.org/external/pubs/ft/wp/2010/wp10244.pdf. [Accessed 1 September 2018].

Muñoz de Bustillo, R. and Antón, J. I. (2012). From the highest employment growth to the deepest fall: Economic crisis and labour inequalities in Spain. In D. Vaughan-Whitehead, ed., *Inequalities in the World of Work: The Effects of the Crisis*. Geneva: ILO, pp. 397–448.

Naude, M., Dickie, C. and Butler, B. (2012). Global economic crisis: Employee responses and practical implications for organisations. *Organisation Development Journal*, 30(4): pp. 9–24.

Nijssen, M. and Paauwe, J. (2012). HRM in turbulent times: How to achieve organisational agility? *The International Journal of Human Resource Management*, 23(16): pp. 3315–3335.

OECD (2008). *Impact of the economic crisis on employment and unemployment in the OECD countries*. [online]. Available at: www.oecd.org/els/emp/impactoftheeconomiccrisisonemploymentandunemploymentintheoecdcountries.htm. [Accessed 6 April 2018].

OECD (2009). *The impact of the global crisis on SME and entrepreneurship financing and policy responses*. [online]. Available at: www.oecd.org/cfe/smes/43183090.pdf. [Accessed 1 September 2018].

OECD (2016a). *OECD economic surveys – Greece – March 2016 overview*. [online]. Available at: www.oecd.org/eco/surveys/economic-survey-greece.htm. [Accessed 15 March 2016].

OECD (2016b). *OECD statistics*. [online]. Available at: http://stats.oecd.org/#. [Accessed 15 March 2016].

Ortega, E. and Penalosa, J. (2012). *The Spanish economic crisis: Key factors and growth challenges in the Euro area.* Documentos Ocasionales, No. 1201, Banco De España.

Pasquino, G. (2008). The 2008 Italian national elections: Berlusconi's third victory. *South European Society and Politics*, 13(3): pp. 345–362.

Price, L., Rae, D. and Cini, V. (2013). SME perceptions of and responses to the recession. *Journal of Small Business and Enterprise Development*, 20(3): pp. 484–502.

Prouska, R. and Kapsali, M. (2011). *Business and Management Practices in Greece: A Comparative Context.* London: Palgrave Macmillan.

Prouska, R. and Psychogios, A. G. (2018a). Do not say a word! Conceptualising employee silence in a long-term crisis context. *The International Journal of Human Resource Management*, 29(5): pp. 885–914.

Prouska, R. and Psychogios, A. G. (2018b). Should I say something? A framework for understanding silence from a line manager's perspective during an economic crisis. *Economic and Industrial Democracy.* doi:10.1177/0143831X17752869.

Prout, M. (2009). Repairing relationships and restoring trust: Behavioral finance and the economic crisis. *Journal of Financial Service Professionals*, 63(4): pp. 75–84.

Psillaki, M. and Eleftheriou, K. (2015). Trade credit, bank credit, and flight to quality: Evidence from French SMEs. *Journal of Small Business Management*, 53: pp. 1219–1240.

Psychogios, A. G. and Wood, G. (2010). Human resource management in Greece in comparative perspective: Alternative institutionalist perspectives and empirical realities. *The International Journal of Human Resource Management*, 21(14): pp. 2614–2630.

Psychogios, A. G., Brewster, C. and Parry, E. (2016). Western European HRM: Reactions and adjustment to crises. In M. Dickmann, C. Brewster and P. Sparrow, eds., *International Human Resource Management: Contemporary Issues in Europe.* (3rd edition). London: Routledge, pp.115–134.

Psychogios, A. G., Szamosi, T. L. and Brewster, C. (2015). Work organisation, human resource management and the economic crisis. In C. F. Machado and J. P. Davim, eds., *Human Resource Management Challenges and Changes.* New York: Nova Science Publishers.

Psychogios, A. G., Theodorakopoulos, N., Nyfoudi, M., Szamosi, T. L. and Prouska, R. (2017). Many hands lighter work? Deciphering the relationship between adverse working conditions and organisational citizenship behaviour in SMEs during an economic crisis. *British Journal of Management.* Early View, First Published 03 November 2017. DOI: 10.1111/1467-8551.12245

Regalia, I. and Regini, M. (2018). Trade unions and employment relations in Italy during the economic crisis. *South European Society and Politics*, 23(1): pp. 63–79.

Reid, G. (2007). *The Foundations of Small Business Enterprises.* London: Routledge.

Rigby, M. and Sanz, Y. P. (2016). International briefing 34: Training and development in Spain. *International Journal of Training & Development*, 20(4): pp. 302–314.

Roche, K. W., Teague, P. and Coughlan, A. (2011). *Human Resources in the Recession: Managing and Representing People at Work in Ireland.* Final Report, Labour Relations Commission.

Rosen, C. C., Halbesleben, J. B. and Perrewe, P. L. (2012). *The Role of the Economic Crisis on Occupational Stress and Well Being.* Bingley: Emerald Group Publishing Limited.

Ruiz, A. C. (2018). Intergenerational occupational dynamics before and during the recent crisis in Spain. *Empirica,* 45(2): pp. 367–393.

Russell, H. and McGinnity, F. (2014). Under pressure: The impact of recession on employees in Ireland. *British Journal of Industrial Relations,* 52: pp. 286–307.

Salimi, M. (2015). *Does low access to finance in Italian SMEs really matter to rampant unemployment?* [online]. Available at: http://englishbulletin.adapt. it/wp-content/uploads/2015/04/Salimi-27-4-2015.pdf.

Samitas, A. and Polyzos, S. (2016). Freeing Greece from capital controls: Were the restrictions enforced in time? *Research in International Business and Finance,* 37(May): pp. 196–213. doi:10.1016/j.ribaf.2015.11.005.

Sanchez-Sellero, M. C. and Sanchez-Sellero, P. (2017). Job satisfaction in Spain: Analysis of the factors in the economic crisis of 2008. *Revija za Socijalnu Politiku,* 24(3): pp. 277–300.

Sani, G. M. D. (2018). The economic crisis and changes in work-family arrangements in six European countries. *Journal of European Social Policy,* 28(2): pp. 177–193.

Sharmila, A. and Gopalakrishnan, K. (2013). An implementation of talent management on SMEs. *Global Management Review,* 7(2): pp. 40–43.

Shoss, M. K. and Probst, T. (2012). Multilevel outcomes of economic stress: An agenda for future research. In P. Perrewe, C. Rosen and J. Halbesleben, eds., *Research in Occupational Stress and Well-being: The Role of Economic Context on Occupational Stress and Well-being.* Bingley: Emerald Group Publishing, Vol. 10, pp. 43–86.

Smallbone, D., Deakins, D., Battisti, M. and Kitching, J. (2012). Small business responses to a major economic downturn: Empirical perspectives from New Zealand and the United Kingdom. *International Small Business Journal,* 30(7): pp. 754–777.

Spreitzer, M. and Mishra, K. (2002). To stay or to go: Voluntary survivor turnover following an organisational downsizing. *Journal of Organisational Behaviour,* 23(6): pp. 707–729.

Stokes, P., Liu, Y., Smith, S., Leidner, S., Moore, N. and Rowland, C. (2016). Managing talent across advanced and emerging economies: HR issues and challenges in a Sino-German strategic collaboration. *International Journal of Human Resource Management,* 27(20): pp. 2310–2338.

Tetlow, G. (2017). *Global economic recovery 'broad-based and stable'.* Financial Times. [online]. Available at: www.ft.com/content/fb29f92e-2022-11e7-b7d3-163f5a7f229c. [Accessed 1 September 2018].

Trading Economics (2018a). *Spain unemployment rate 1976–2018.* [online]. Available at: https://tradingeconomics.com/spain/unemployment-rate.

Trading Economics (2018b). *Spain youth unemployment rate 1986–2018.* [online]. Available at: https://tradingeconomics.com/spain/youth-unemployment-rate.

Wallace, J. and O'Sullivan, M. (2006). Contemporary strike trends since 1980: Peering through the wrong end of a telescope. In M. J. Morley, P. Gunnigle and D. G. Collings, eds., *Global Industrial Relations.* London: Routledge, pp. 273–291.

Williams, N. and Vorley, T. (2015). The impact of institutional change on entrepreneurship in a crisis-hit economy: The case of Greece. *Entrepreneurship and Regional Development*, 27(1–2): pp. 28–49. doi:10.1080/08985626.2014.995723.

Wood, G., Szamosi, L. T., Psychogios, A. G., Sarvanidis, S. and Fotopoulou, D. (2015). Rethinking Greek capitalism through the lens of industrial relations reform: A view until the 2015 referendum. *Relations Industrielles/Industrial Relations Quarterly Review*, 70(4): pp. 698–717.

8 Conclusion

Overview

The purpose of this book was to explore empirical evidence related to HRM application in SMEs that operate in turbulent contexts. By using the term 'turbulence', we refer to an entire process of continued and long-term economic shift of a country, characterised by high levels of uncertainty, volatility and structural change. The term is used to describe various economies that are either in development, transformation, transition or crisis. In our approach, we have used the term to describe three similar types of turbulence: EMEs, transition economies and crisis economies.

EMEs refer to those economies that are progressing towards becoming more developed. They achieve this progression mainly by transforming their economic aspects following a liberalisation and deregulation logic, such as increased market orientation, rapid growth and the expansion of their economic foundation. At the same time, they maintain institutional logics, such as informality. We have included in this category countries from Asia and the Pacific, Africa and Latin America. For many researchers, countries in Eastern and South-Eastern Europe are also included in this category. Nevertheless, in this book, we have classified the latter as transition economies. These countries share some similar features with EMEs. They have been in a process of economic transition from communist regimes to capitalist since the beginning of the 1990s. These countries used to belong either to the USSR block or to the Yugoslav state. The long transition process in these countries includes, among other things, the removal of trade barriers, privatisation of state-owned enterprises, emergence of various businesses and an establishment of a new financial system that facilitates private investments. The third type of turbulence refers to developed economies that either have passed through financial crisis or are still in financial crisis (at the time of writing). In Europe, the impact of the crisis varied considerably between EU member states. It seems that its impact was more substantial in the South rather than in the North, resulting in critical changes in countries like Greece, Italy and Spain. These countries implemented the largest austerity cuts, with negative implications for organisations and employees.

Beyond the focus on turbulent contexts, this book also focused on SMEs. The OECD defines SMEs as organisations with less than 500 employees. Given that this book focused on turbulent economies across regions characterised by organisations of varying size, we adopted this broader approach to the SME definition. It is widely known that SMEs are fundamental for the development of every country, but their importance is even more critical for emerging, transition and crisis economies. SMEs expand productive capability and help absorb productive resources at all levels of the economy. This creates flexibility in economic systems that allows collaboration between small and large companies. Especially in turbulent contexts, SMEs can enhance changes and modernise the system. SMEs absorb both material and human resources from larger firms while they reformulate labour market conditions, ensuring a balancing process between them and larger companies. SMEs are embedded in the institutional structures of emerging economies, by contributing to the economic development through employment opportunities for growth of the rural and urban labour force. However, there are still many challenges that SMEs face, especially in turbulent economies. A major challenge relates to the management of human resources. Human resources are considered extremely important for SMEs, since such resources can provide the appropriate competitive advantage through their knowledge and experience, especially when these companies do not have the ability to invest in developing new technologies and innovations.

SMEs generally rely on informal HRM practices. This informality has been attributed partly to the owner's role in HRM decisions, given the lack of formal HRM investment in small settings. Even when organisational size permits the presence of HRM specialists, it is still the owner, or managing director, who is generally seen to be in charge of HRM, while HRM specialists are often seen to deal with administrative rather than strategic tasks. In terms of the core HR functions, recruitment and selection is the most utilised practice compared to the other functions. The recruitment and selection practice in small firms relies heavily on word of mouth and references. Given the preference for informality in these firms, it is quite rare to find formal role descriptions and selection procedures being used in these firms. Moreover, training and development in SMEs is often informal and short-term oriented. Arguably, the type of work in SMEs does not lend itself to formalised off-site training, which has the potential to enhance employee performance. In terms of employee relations, it is important to acknowledge the fact that SMEs exhibit great diversity among themselves but also in comparison with larger firms in many ways. It is rare to find trade unions or collective bargaining present in SMEs or to find large internal labour markets. Decision-making in these small firms is usually centralised. The culture in these firms is typically moulded by the owner/CEO, who communicates organisational objectives directly to employees. This creates an informal and flexible working environment. However, it seems the development of HRM practices is not occurring at the same level in all SMEs operating in turbulent contexts. In this respect, this book attempted to map the current state of affairs of HRM in SMEs in these contexts.

Current State of Affairs of HRM in SMEs in Turbulent Contexts

This book explored how the application of HRM in SMEs in turbulent contexts followed similar logics to more developed economies. EMEs in Asia and the Pacific are undergoing a transition. This transition is influenced by historical, cultural and institutional factors, which determine the way in which HRM is implemented. In addition, it seems that both SME size and sector play a significant role in the adoption of HRM practices. Chinese SMEs have undergone a formalisation process of HRM and employment practices mainly due to the internationalisation of businesses in recent years. For example, the external focus of Chinese local manufacturers press them to adopt some formal HR methods. In addition, both Chinese culture and institutions seem to influence the application of Western-type HR practices. Similarly, Indian SMEs are progressively applying HRM practices, such as training and talent management. However, strong cultural and institutional aspects determine HR application. In other countries of Asia, like Taiwan, HRM application is limited due to cultural factors and to the high proportion of family-owned enterprises that rely on informal systems of management. Moreover, in other countries, like Vietnam, HRM application in SMEs depends upon pressures emerging from international competition, state-owned enterprises, expectations from international business partners and customers. Finally, in some other countries, like South Korea, there is evidence of HRM practices applied by SMEs, albeit not consistently across organisations.

Similar features have been observed through our analysis of SMEs in emerging economies located in Africa. Although there is limited reliable data for the countries in this region, there is some evidence regarding some of them, namely South Africa, Ghana, Nigeria and Algeria. South African SMEs emphasise the need for enhancing their competitiveness, managerial skills, training and retention strategies for skilled workers. In addition, Ghanaian SMEs apply some core HR practices, such as recruitment, selection and training. Other HR activities, such as reward management, performance management, talent management and HR development, are considered as less strategic and, therefore, less important to consistently apply. In Nigeria, SMEs depict a mix of HRM formality and informality depending on their industry. In addition, historical and institutional factors have affected HRM practices. Similar factors that have shaped HRM application in SMEs can be observed in

Algeria. For example, recruitment and selection practices in this context are mainly influenced by networking and nepotism.

The last two emerging economies examined in this book are Chile and Colombia, both of which belong to the Latin American context. There was limited evidence about HRM in SMEs in other countries of Latin America. As far as Chile and Colombia are concerned, HRM logics are based on particular historical developments in both countries, particularly the transition of their political regimes. Furthermore, strong institutional influences, such as globalised market demands, press SMEs to modernise HR management practices. Similarly, specific cultural aspects, such as the authoritarian management style, seem to be dominant in many Latin American organisations and define the way in which HR practices are applied in SMEs. HRM is heavily dependent on top management decision-making in SMEs.

HRM in transition economies of Eastern Europe exhibits some similarities with HRM in EMEs in Asia, Africa and Latin America. The ex-communist and autarchic environment of state control in these countries had a negative impact on entrepreneurial development and FDI. MNCs operating in transition economies influence management thinking and practices of local SMEs. In addition, the management style of SME owners affects informality of practices in these organisations. Unregulated economic activities are a common feature in this region. Our analysis suggested that SMEs in transition economies do not have formalised HRM functions, but we noted the influence of the specific business context in which SMEs operate. In particular, we found three factors affecting the formalisation of HRM practice in SMEs operating in a post-communist context: degree of internationalisation, sector and size. In other words, SMEs in transition economies tend to adopt formal HR practices either because they are growing in size or because they are expanding internationally. Finally, SMEs in the manufacturing sector seem to be keener to apply a range of HRM practices.

The last turbulent context that we explored was the one that emerged in some European economies after the 2008 global financial crisis. We examined three EU countries that were severely affected by the crisis: Greece, Italy and Spain. SMEs in these countries were vulnerable during the crisis due to a weak resource base in terms of financial capital, human capital, HR expertise, and network and market power. These factors did not enable SMEs in this context to possess discretion and options over strategic choices and responses during recession. SMEs are generally more vulnerable in times of crisis for a variety of reasons: inability to downsize, as they are already small; less diversification in their economic activities; weaker financial structures; lower or no credit rating; heavy dependence on credit; and fewer financing options. We have seen that in the three European countries under exploration, SMEs struggled to overcome the economic crisis due to their inability to downsize and diversify products/services, their weak financial structures and their limited access to finance. As a response to these impediments, SMEs had to cut labour costs by freezing recruitment, downsizing and implementing pay cuts and layoffs. This context led to the intensification of adverse working conditions for employees in SMEs making their working lives prone to job insecurity, work intensification and pressure. As a result, employee productivity, loyalty and commitment exhibited a decline. SMEs need strategies to retain engagement and performance levels, particularly in order to maintain levels of employee engagement in this challenging context.

Towards an Emergent Conceptual Model of HRM in SMEs in Turbulent Contexts

This book dealt with HRM issues in SMEs in turbulent economies by emphasising coordination or congruence among the various HRM practices. It focused on the HRM orientation of SMEs as a general approach initiated and followed by owners and top managers in these companies. Our analysis was based on reliable and valid evidence found about three different types of turbulent economies: emerging markets, transition economies and economies under financial crisis. Building on this literature, as well as on empirical data from authors with published research in the field, we propose a conceptual model for HRM practices in SMEs in turbulent economies that includes two main constructs: macro and micro. We found that both groups of constructs shape HR strategy development and execution in SMEs. The model, as seen in Figure 8.1, considers all relevant links between these constructs.

The logic of the macro and micro constructs of the model is to incorporate factors both external and internal to the organisation that facilitate or inhibit the application of HRM practices in SMEs. The internal factors (micro level) directly affect HR strategy development and HR strategy execution, while the external factors (macro level) influence the overall dynamic of HR implementation. In particular, this model suggests that HRM in SMEs in turbulent contexts is formulated on an *ad hoc* and emergent basis. The macro-level construct consists of two main factors. The first is the cultural context of each turbulent economy. The second is the historical and institutional context of the country. The latter includes various aspects that influence the way that managers decide upon HR strategies as well as the way in which they implement them. For example, power distance is a dominant cultural factor that influences not only the decision on the type of HR practices to be applied but also the decision on how HR practices are applied, with a direct impact on the effectiveness of these HR practices. This factor is linked to both historical aspects of SMEs' development in these economies, as well as on the family-oriented nature of many SMEs that follow a more

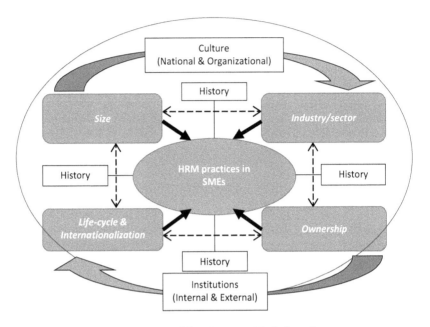

Figure 8.1 Emergent HRM Model in SMEs in Turbulent Contexts.

paternalistic approach to managing people. Uncertainty avoidance is another cultural factor affecting HRM adoption. In fact, many companies attempting to control their processes and employee behaviour are keener to adopt more sophisticated management practices, like those suggested by HRM experts. The target is to reduce uncertainty emerging from the expansion of processes and procedures within SMEs. In contrast, other SMEs in turbulent economies tend to be less keen to adopt long-term HR strategies since they are governed by a short-term cultural orientation.

These cultural factors are enhanced, in most cases, by historical aspects. For instance, the autocratic organisational environment that dominated for decades in post-communist countries seems to facilitate the top-down features of the HRM strategies in SMEs in these contexts. In other words, the recent political and economic history of these counties formulated various institutions which, in turn, affected business development. For instance, the economic development of these countries seems to determine SMEs' effectiveness. This in turn can influence SMEs' decisions regarding people management policies. Another internal institutional factor that is evident in the countries we examined relates to government policies that favour entrepreneurial activity of small companies. There are countries where there are specific regulatory aspects facilitating or prohibiting such activity. An example can be found by looking at employee relations and employee voice within

SMEs. Usually, in turbulent economic systems, employee relations are less supported by the state through regulatory actions. Thus, you can hardly find organised and strong trade unions in SMEs that could potentially lead to formal HRM adoption.

Beyond the internal institutional factors, one can observe a series of external ones that have a great degree of influence towards SMEs' willingness to apply HRM practices. The most important of these factors is the presence of MNCs in these countries, particularly when MNCs interact with local SMEs. Usually, MNCs have the negotiation power and require specific standards of operation from SMEs in order to approve collaboration. In many cases, this pressure leads SMEs to adopt HRM practices in order to enhance the collaboration. In general, HRM strategies that MNCs apply act as prototypes for imitation for SMEs. A mimetic aspect of HR adoption is observed especially in emergent markets, as well as economies in transition. Further to the presence of MNCs, there are strong indirect institutional influences that emerge from international organisations and political bodies. For example, the presence of the IMF in some transition economies and economies under crisis has driven the process of economic deregulation, which in turn has affected small companies that have fewer means of survival. Automatically, this has an impact on the adoption of HR strategies. Finally, political entities like the EU can also have a direct impact on SMEs' growth and an indirect impact on HRM in SMEs. For example, SMEs in transition or crisis economies that are EU members can be eligible to apply for EU funding when they fulfil specific standards of eligibility. Part of these standards is related to specific management practices (including HRM) that demonstrate the SMEs' ability to operate effectively and efficiently.

The macro-level factors mentioned earlier can be seen and understood in relation to the micro-level factors. Our investigation came up with four specific micro-level factors that affect HR application in SMEs in turbulent economic contexts. The first micro-level factor is the industry/sector that the company belongs to. Our evidence showed that manufacturing companies are more willing to implement HR strategies and adopt a more formal or sophisticated approach to HR. In contrast, SMEs belonging to other types of industries, such as services and retail, seem to be less motivated to adopt a formal HRM approach. However, this fact seems to be moderated by a series of other micro-level factors. The second micro-level factor is organisational size. As we have seen in this book, SMEs decide to become more HR-oriented organisations as they grow in size. This is logical, since the larger the company, the bigger the need to control procedures and processes among staff. Therefore, the larger SMEs tend to be keener on the adoption of formal HR practices, and this seems to be the rule in turbulent economies as well. The third micro-level factor is the life-cycle stage of the company. In particular, we have found that SMEs that expand internationally, either through enhancing exports and international collaborations or through establishing subsidiaries in other countries, tend to formalise HR. This, for example, seems to be the case in many organisations in the transition economies of Eastern Europe, but also in organisations in large emerging economies such as China and India. The fourth micro-level factor is associated with SME ownership. The analysis provided evidence suggesting that when companies are under the control of a single family, HR adoption heavily depends on the family members that usually staff top management positions in their firms. There are cases where family-owned SMEs are keen to adopt HRM practices, but family values frequently take precedent. SMEs with shareholders usually apply formal HR strategies as a means of following procedures and maintaining internal control.

Drawing from the earlier description of the model, we can argue that if we want to understand the nature of HRM in SMEs in turbulent contexts, we need to first understand the path that these SMEs follow in order to apply HR strategies and practices. In other words, there is a type of path dependency in the application of HR in these SMEs that consists of both macro-level factors and micro-level ones. It is critical to state that both groups of factors need to be seen as interconnected and interrelated. In short, we cannot separate them and study them independently from one another if we want to capture the essence of understanding HRM in SMEs in these contexts.

Practical Implications, Further Research & Final Thoughts

In this book, we strongly argued and supported the view that SMEs are at the core of turbulent economies, and, therefore, there is a need to support the development of such enterprises. A purpose of this book was to contribute in this direction. In other words, we were interested in understanding the context of turbulent business environments that SMEs operate in and attempted to comprehend how HRM is applied in these contexts. Our objective was to find ways to support these organisations to survive and grow. Managing people in SMEs is a critical aspect of survival and growth. Therefore, SMEs in turbulent economies need to be further understood and supported in applying realistic management practices. They should not be encouraged to copy methods applied in MNCs. We argue that HR practices need to be contextualised and understood within the particular factors (macro and micro) of the context that SMEs operate in. At the same time, SME managers and owners need to develop their understanding of these contexts. A simple, but holistic, framework can help them towards this direction. SME managers need to learn to live and expand within the formality-informality continuum while developing their capability to understand which HR practices should be formalised.

Therefore, there is a need for a more holistic approach to research on HRM in SMEs in turbulent economies, one that will take into consideration both macro and micro contextual factors. This study offered a holistic and interconnected conceptual framework that attempts to illustrate the main factors determining the context of application of HRM in SMEs in turbulent business systems. Without a doubt, more studies are needed to either confirm the proposed factors (macro and micro level) or expand these factors. Moreover, there is a need for country-specific studies referring to particular regions. At the moment, there is scarcity of research in several regions, such as Latin America, Africa and Asia. In addition, more comparative studies between turbulent economies, as well as between turbulent and more 'stable' ones, would help us better comprehend the similarities and differences between cultural and institutional contexts. Future studies about HRM in SMEs in turbulent contexts need to take into account sectoral variables as well as differences in ownership. Finally, more research is needed to holistically explore convergence versus divergence of HRM practices in SMEs in these economies.

Despite the aforementioned suggestions, we strongly believe that our conceptual framework provides a coherent and concrete foundation for further research in the field. Our proposed framework is based on simplicity and adopts a broad approach that not only includes the key factors, such as cultural, institutional and organisational, but also the interplay between them.

Overall, for a long period of time, management thinking and practice, including HRM, has been dominated by Western approaches usually developed and tested in large multinational corporations. It is clear now that there is no global (mainly US-oriented) management approach to businesses and people. The new idea is to explore management practices, including HRM, in context. In this respect, exploring and understanding the underestimated context of SMEs, as well as turbulent (emergent, transition and crisis) economies around the world, can add a great deal of knowledge and enhance our understanding of how SMEs manage their processes and people. It is time to remove the blinkers and develop new HRM theories and practices that are not following the traditional (Western) management jargon but that are built on the special features of every single context.

Index

For Product Safety Concerns and Information please contact our EU
representative GPSR@taylorandfrancis.com
Taylor & Francis Verlag GmbH, Kaufingerstraße 24, 80331 München, Germany

www.ingramcontent.com/pod-product-compliance
Ingram Content Group UK Ltd.
Pitfield, Milton Keynes, MK11 3LW, UK
UKHW020945180425
457613UK00019B/523